The Queen and I

Sue Townsend lives in Leicester. Her published work includes *The Secret Diary of Adrian Mole Aged 13³/4; The Growing Pains of Adrian Mole; The True Confessions of Adrian Albert Mole, Margaret Hilda Roberts and Susan Lilian Townsend* and *Adrian Mole: From Minor to Major*. Her novel, *Rebuilding Coventry*, was published in 1985. Her playe include *Womberang* (Soho Poly, London, 1979), *Bazaar and Rummage* (Royal Court Theatre Upstairs, 1982; BBC Television 1983); *The Great Celestial Cow* (Royal Court 1984); *Disneyland It Ain't* (Royal Court Theatre Upstairs, 1988) and *Ten Tiny Fingers, Nine Tiny Toes* (Library Theatre, Manchester, 1989).

SUE TOWNSEND

The Queen and I

Mandarin

With drawings by Martin Honeysett

A Mandarin Paperback
THE QUEEN AND I

First published in Great Britain 1992
by Methuen London
This edition published 1993
by Mandarin Paperbacks
an imprint of Reed Consumer Books Ltd
Michelin House, 81 Fulham Road, London SW3 6RB
and Auckland, Melbourne, Singapore and Toronto

Copyright © 1992 by Sue Townsend
The author has asserted her moral rights

A CIP catalogue record for this title
is available from the British Library
ISBN 0 7493 1352 8

Printed in Great Britain
by Cox & Wyman Ltd, Reading, Berks

For Gabrielle, Bailey and Niall

AUTHOR'S NOTE

The Queen and I is a work of fiction.
Names, characters, places and incidents either
are the product of the author's imagination
or are used entirely fictitiously.

Contents

Now, when thou wak'st, with thine
own fool's eyes peek

William Shakespeare, *A Midsummer Night's Dream*

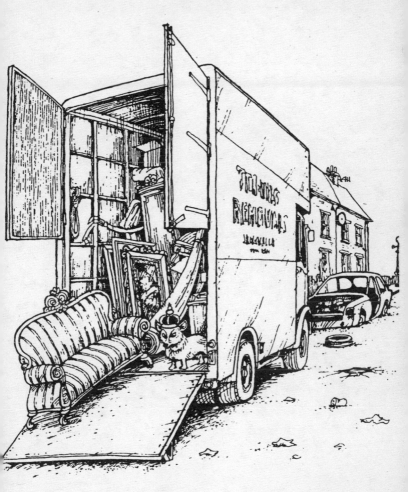

1 Uneasy Lies the Head

The Queen was in bed watching television with Harris. It was election night, 11.20 pm, Thursday 9 April 1992. Harris yawned, displaying his sharp teeth and liver-coloured tongue.

'Are you bored with the election, my darling?' asked the Queen, stroking Harris's back.

Harris barked at the television, where a display of computer graphics (little men in top hats) was jerking about on the screen. The Queen watched with amused incomprehension for a while, before realising that the red, blue and orange computer men represented the present composition of the House of Commons. A tall man with flailing arms stood in front of the display and gabbled about the accuracy of opinion polls and the likelihood of a hung parliament. The Queen reached for the remote control and turned the volume down. She recalled how, earlier in the day, a secretary had passed her a clipping from a Conservative newspaper, saying, 'This may amuse you, Ma'am.'

It certainly had amused her. A spirit medium employed by the paper had claimed to have been in touch with Stalin, Hitler and Ghengis Khan, who had all assured the medium that, given the opportunity, they would have been hot-footing it to the polling stations and voting Labour. She had shown the clipping to Philip at dinner, but he hadn't seen the joke.

Harris grumbled in the back of his throat, jumped out of bed and waddled over to the television set. It was now 11.25 pm. Harris barked angrily at the screen as the result for Basildon was declared. The Queen lay back on her crisp linen pillows and wondered who would be kissing her hand tomorrow afternoon, nice John Major or perfectly agreeable Neil Kinnock. She had no particular preference. Both party leaders publicly supported the monarchy and neither was Mrs Thatcher, whose mad eyes and strangulated voice had quite unnerved the Queen at their regular Tuesday afternoon meetings. The Queen wondered if the day would ever dawn when a victorious Prime Minister did *not* support the monarchy.

The computer men vanished from the screen to be replaced yet again by anxious politicians being interviewed and Harris lost interest and jumped back onto the bed. After turning full circle, he settled himself onto the downy softness of the bedcover and lay down. The Queen reached out and patted him goodnight. She removed her glasses, pressed the 'off' button on the remote control, then lay in the darkness and waited for sleep. Family worries came crowding into her mind. The Queen whispered the prayer that Crawfie, her governess, had taught her, over sixty years ago:

> If I should die before I wake
> I pray the Lord my soul to take.

As she took her last conscious breath before sleep overtook her, the Queen wondered what would happen

to her and her family if a Republican Government were
to be elected: it was the Queen's nightmare.

2 A Breath of Air

The Queen winced as Jack Barker ground his cigarette out on the silk rug. A faint smell of burning rose between them. Jack fought the urge to apologise. The Queen stared at Jack disdainfully. His stomach gurgled. Her picture had hung in his classroom when he was struggling to learn his nine times tables. In his boyhood he used to look to the Queen for inspiration. Prince Charles bent down and picked up the cigarette stub. He looked for somewhere to put it, but, finding nowhere suitable, he slipped it into his pocket.

Princess Margaret said, 'Lilibet I've *got* to have a fag. Please!'

'May we open the windows, Mr Barker?' asked the Queen. Her accent cut into Jack like a crystal. He half expected to bleed.

'No chance,' he replied.

'Am I to have a house of my own, Mr Barker, or must I share with my daughter and son-in-law?' The Queen Mother gave Jack her famous smile, but her hands were twisting the full skirt of her periwinkle dress into a knot.

'You'll get a pensioner's bungalow. It's your entitlement as an ordinary citizen of this country.'

'A bungalow, good. I couldn't manage stairs. Will my staff be living in or out?'

Jack laughed and looked at his fellow Republicans. Six men and six women, hand-picked to witness this historic occasion. They laughed along with Jack.

'You don't seem to understand. There'll be no staff, no dressers, no cooks, secretaries, cleaners, chauffeurs.'

Turning to the Queen he said, 'You'll have to nip in now and then, help your mum out. But she'll probably be entitled to Meals on Wheels.'

The Queen Mother looked quite pleased to hear this. 'So I shan't starve?'

'Under the People's Republican Party's rule, nobody in Britain will starve,' said Jack.

Prince Charles cleared his throat and said, 'Er, may one, er, enquire as to where. . . ? That is, the location. . . ?'

'If you're asking me where you're all going, I'm not telling you. All I can say at the moment is that you'll all be in the same street, but you'll have strangers as next-door neighbours, working-class people. Here's a list of what you can take with you.'

Jack held out photocopies of each of the lists his wife had compiled only two hours before. The lists were headed: *Essential Items; Furniture; Fittings, suitable for two-bedroomed council house and pensioner's bungalow.* The Queen Mother's list was much shorter, she noticed. Jack held the papers out, but nobody came forward to take them. Jack didn't move. He knew that one of them would crack. Eventually Diana got up, she hated scenes. She took the papers from Jack and gave each member of the Royal Family their list. There was quiet for a few moments while they read. Jack fiddled with the gun in his pocket. Only he knew that it wasn't loaded.

'Mr Barker, there is no mention of dogs here,' said the Queen.

'One per family,' said Jack.

'Horses?' asked Charles.

'Would you keep a horse in a council house garden?'

'No. Quite. One wasn't thinking.'

'Clothes aren't on the list,' said Diana, shyly.

'You won't be needing much. Just the bare essentials. You won't be making personal appearances, will you?'

Princess Anne rose and stood next to her father. 'Thank God for that! At least something good has come out of this bloody shambles. Are you all right, Pa?'

Prince Philip was in a state of shock and had been ever since the previous night when he had turned on the television for Election Night Special at 11.25 and seen the announcement of the election of Jack Barker, founder and leader of the People's Republican Party, as the member for Kensington West. Prince Philip had watched incredulously as Barker had addressed the joyous crowds in the Town Hall. Middle-aged poll tax payers had cheered alongside young people wearing ragged jeans and nose rings. He had lifted the telephone and advised his wife to watch the television set. Half an hour later, she rang him back. 'Philip, please come to my room.'

They had sat up until the early hours as one Republican candidate after another had been declared elected in front of cheering crowds of British citizenry.

Gradually their children had joined them. At 7.30 am the servants brought them breakfast, but nobody ate. By 11 am the People's Republican Party had won 451 seats and John Major, the Conservative Prime Minister, had reluctantly conceded defeat. Shortly afterwards, Jack Barker announced that he was Prime Minister. His first job, he said, would be to go to Buckingham Palace and order the Queen to abdicate.

The thirteen Republicans in a minibus had been waved through the gates of Buckingham Palace by smiling policemen. The soldiers of the Household Cavalry had removed their bearskins and waved them in the air. Members of the Queen's personal staff had shaken them by the hand. Champagne had been offered, but had been declined.

Until his election as member for Kensington West, Jack Barker had been the leader of a breakaway section of the Television Technicians' Union. For the three weeks preceding the General Election, Jack and his disgruntled members had broadcast subliminal messages to the watching public: 'VOTE REPUBLICAN – END THE MONARCHY'.

On the Saturday before polling day, *The Times* had called for the dismantling of the monarchy. A hundred thousand anti-monarchists had walked from Trafalgar Square to Clarence House, not knowing that the Queen Mother was at the races. A violent thunderstorm had dispersed them before she returned, but she saw the discarded placards from the window of her limousine.

'GOD DAMN YOU MA'AM'

An error, she thought, surely they *meant* 'God Bless', didn't they?

That evening, she noticed that her staff were surly and uncooperative. She'd had to wait half an hour for a servant to draw her bedroom curtains.

On polling day the British people, brainwashed by the television technicians, had made their choice.

An officer of the Household Cavalry knocked and then came into the room.

'They're calling for you, sir,' he said.

Jack snapped, 'Don't call me *sir*, I'm plain Jack Barker to you – right?'

Jack addressed the assembled Royals: 'We're going on the balcony for a breath of air.'

The walk from the back of the palace to the front made Jack breathless; he was out of condition. It was a long time since he'd walked so far.

'How many rooms have you got?' he found himself asking the Queen as they trudged along the endless corridors.

'Enough,' said the Queen.

'Four hundred and thirty-nine, we think,' said Charles helpfully.

As they turned a corner a low grumbling growl could be heard, as though a hibernating bear were being prodded awake with a stick. As the Republicans and the Royals entered the Centre Room the noise overwhelmed them. When Jack Barker stepped out onto the balcony the crowd below opened their throats and roared, 'Jack, Jack, send 'em back!'

Jack looked down at the citizenry of Great Britain

surrounding the palace. The Mall and the Parks were so full of bodies that not an inch of pavement or a blade of grass could be seen. He was now responsible for their food, their education, their drains – and finding the money to pay for it all. Could he do it? Was he up to it? How long would they give him to prove himself?

Above the noise he shouted, 'Would the ex-Royal Family join me, please?'

The Queen straightened her back, adjusted the handbag on her arm and stepped onto the balcony. When the vast crowd saw the small familiar figure they grew silent, then, like children defying a stern parent, they again began to roar, 'Jack, Jack, send 'em back.'

As the other ex-Royals filed onto the balcony the boos and catcalls began. Diana tried to hold her husband's hand but he frowned and put his hands behind his back. Princess Margaret lit a cigarette and inserted it into a tortoiseshell holder. Prince Philip and the Princess Royal linked arms, as though the noise of the crowd were tangible and would knock them off their feet.

The Queen Mother smiled and waved as was her habit. She was too old to change now. She longed for a gin and tonic. It wasn't her custom to drink before lunch, but this was rather a special day. She would ask Mr Barker if it was possible when they had finished this rather disagreeable duty.

One of the Republicans handed Jack a Safeways plastic bag. It contained something heavy and bulky. The bottom of the bag strained to contain its burden.

Two Republicans held the bag open and Jack removed the Imperial State Crown. It was bordered with pearls and set with glowing clusters of emeralds, sapphires and diamonds. Jack turned the crown around so that the Black Prince's Ruby faced the crowd. He then held it over his head with his arms fully stretched and hurled it into the courtyard below. As it fell, the Queen recollected how she had hated and feared that crown. In the days before her coronation she had dreamed of the crown falling from her head as she rose from the throne. Now, as she watched her household staff scrambling for the scattered gems in the courtyard below, she remembered the nervous breath of the Archbishop of Canterbury as he had placed the seven pound crown on her head.

'Wave goodbye,' instructed Jack Barker.

The ex-Royal Family waved, each remembering happier occasions, wedding dresses, kisses, the cheers of the adoring crowds. They turned and went inside. Now it was Jack and his colleagues who were cheered until the pictures on the palace walls vibrated. Jack didn't stay long, he would not encourage the cult of personality. It caused jealousy and resentment; and Jack wanted to keep the affection and respect of his colleagues for as long as possible. He liked being in charge. At infant school he had been the class milk monitor, placing a bottle of milk before each pupil, then making them wait for a straw, then collecting the silver foil tops and pressing them into the large ball they were intending to give to the blind. If a child inadvertently squashed its straw, Jack sternly refused to hand out another.

Five-year-old Jack lived in chaos at home. He liked school because of the rules. When Mrs Biggs, his fat teacher, shouted at him, he felt safe. Jack's mother had never shouted; she hardly spoke to him apart from telling him to go to the shop for five Woodbines.

Inside the Centre Room the Queen waved Margaret's cigarette smoke away and asked, 'How long have we got?'

'Forty-eight hours,' said Jack.

The Queen said, 'That is very short notice, Mr Barker.'

Jack said, 'You should have known your time was up years ago.' To the assembled Royals he said, 'Go to your homes and stay there. You'll be notified of your removal dates.'

To Charles he said, 'Relieved, eh?'

Charles pretended he didn't know what Barker was talking about. He said, 'Mr Barker, may we also move on Sunday? I would like to support my mother.'

'Certainly,' said Jack, sardonically. 'It's your prerogative. Though not, of course, your *royal* prerogative, not any more.'

Charles felt he ought to put up more of a show of resistance in front of his mother, so he said:

'My family have given years of devoted service to this country, my mother in particular. . . .'

'She's been well paid for it,' snapped Jack. 'And I could give you the names of a dozen people I know personally who have worked twice as hard for their country as your mother and have been paid *nowt*.' Jack's use of the word 'nowt' came from his childhood, a time of poverty and humiliation, when his political philosophy was formed.

Prince Charles rubbed the side of his nose with

a manicured forefinger and said, 'But we have per-petuated certain standards. . . .'

Jack was glad they were having this conversation. It was one he had rehearsed in his mind many times.

'What your family has perpetuated,' he said, 'is a hierarchy, with you at the top and others, inevi-tably, below you. Our country is class ridden as a result. Class fear has strangled us, Mr Windsor. Our country has been stagnating at the same rate as your family has been capitalising on its wealth and power. I am merely bringing this imbalance to an end.'

The Queen had listened to enough of this Repub-lican rubbish. She said, 'So you will be scratching around looking for a new figurehead, a president of some kind, will you?'

'No,' said Jack. 'The British people will be their own figurehead, all fifty-seven million of them.'

'Hard to photograph fifty-seven million people,' said the Queen. She opened and then snapped shut her handbag. Jack noticed that it was empty, apart from a white lace handkerchief.

'Do I have your permission to leave?' she said.

'Certainly,' said Jack, with a small incline of the head.

The Queen left the room and walked along the corridors. As she did so, she read the list of things she could take with her and the specifications of her new home.

9 HELLEBORE CLOSE
FLOWERS ESTATE

GENERAL INFORMATION: This two-bedroomed, semi-detached, pre-war property situated in the area of the Flowers Estate, has been recently redecorated throughout and briefly comprises: Front Entrance, Entrance Hall, Lounge, Kitchen, Bathroom, Landing, Two Bedrooms, Boxroom and Separate W.C. To the outside, driveway and front and rear garden.

ACCOMMODATION:

Ground Floor

Front Entrance: with door to entrance hall:
Entrance Hall: with stairs to first floor, storage cupboard.
Lounge: 14′ 10″ × 12′ 7″ with gas fire point.
Kitchen: 9′ 6″ × 9′ 9″ requiring fitments but including sink, gas cooker point and door to rear.
Bathroom: with two-piece suite comprising: cast iron bath, wash hand basin, partly tiled walls, frosted window and boiler.

First Floor

Landing: with access to loft space.
Bedroom 1: 13′ 1″ × 10′ 1″
Bedroom 2: 9′ 5″ × 9′ 2″
Boxroom: 6′ × 6′
Separate W.C.: with low level W.C. and frosted window.

OUTSIDE: The property is approached by pathway with garden and path to side entrance, together with garden to rear.

PLEASE NOTE: We can give no warranty as to whether or not any boiler or heating/water system to the property is operational.

3 Never So Humble

It was dusk when the furniture van drew up outside Number Nine Hellebore Close. The Queen looked stonily at her new home. The house looked grimly back through the gloom, as though it bore a grudge. Its windows were boarded. Somebody violent and strong had driven in six-inch nails and connected hardboard panels to the window frames. A small sycamore tree was growing from the upstairs guttering.

The Queen adjusted her headscarf and straightened her back. She looked at the mean front door: our furniture will never fit through, she thought, and we will have to share a wall – what was the technical term? Something celebratory. A *party* wall, that was it! The door of Number Eleven opened and a man in a tee shirt and overalls came out and stood on his concrete step. A woman joined him, blonde and fleshy, wearing clothes a size too small and red fluffy mules. The fluff waved about in the evening breeze, looking like creatures on the sea bed searching for plankton.

The man and the woman were husband and wife – Beverley and Tony Threadgold – the Queen's new neighbours. They gawped at the removal van, not bothering to disguise their curiosity. The house next door to them had been empty for over a year so the Threadgolds had enjoyed the luxury of comparative privacy. They'd shouted, banged doors and made love without vocal restraint, and now it was over. It was a sad day for them. They hoped their new neighbours would be reasonably, but not too, respectable.

The driver of the removal van went round and opened the door for the Queen. She climbed down, grateful for the volume of material in her tweed skirt.

'Come on, Philip,' she encouraged, but Philip sat on, in the front of the van, clutching his briefcase to him, as though it were a hot water bottle and he were a hypothermia victim.

'Philip, this gentleman has a family to go home to.'

The driver was pleased to be called a gentleman by the Queen.

'No 'urry,' he said, graciously.

But in truth he couldn't wait to get back to his own council house, to tell his wife about the journey up the M1. About how he and the Queen had talked of homeopathic medicine and dogs and the problems of adolescent children.

'I'll give you an 'and in with your stuff,' he offered.

'How kind, but the Republican Party suggested that my husband and I must get used to coping for ourselves.'

The driver confided, 'Nobody in our house voted for 'em. We always vote Conservative, always.'

The Queen confided, 'Somebody in *our* house supported them.'

The driver nodded towards Prince Philip. 'Not 'im?'

The Queen laughed at the thought.

A second removal van roared into the close. The

doors opened immediately and the Queen's grand-children climbed out. The Queen waved and the little boys ran towards her. Prince Charles helped his wife out of the van. Diana had dressed for adversity: denim and cowboy boots. She looked at Number Eight Hellebore Close and shuddered. But Prince Charles smiled. Here, at last, was the simple life.

4 Poshos

The street sign at the entrance to the Close had lost five black metal letters. HELL   CLOSE it now said, illuminated by the light of a flickering street lamp.

The Queen thought, 'Yes, it *is* Hell, it must be, because I've never seen anything like it in the whole of my waking life.'

She had visited many council estates – had opened community centres, had driven through the bunting and the cheering crowds, alighted from the car, walked on red carpets, been given a posy by a two-year-old in a 'Mothercare' party frock, been greeted by tongue-tied dignitaries, pulled a cord, revealed a plaque, signed the visitors' book. Then, carpet, car, drive to helicopter and up, up and away. She'd seen the odd documentary on BBC2 about urban poverty, heard unattractive poor people talk in broken sentences about their dreadful lives, but she'd regarded such programmes as sociological curiosities, on a par with watching the circumcision ceremonies of Amazonian Indians, so far away that it didn't really matter.

It stank. Somebody in the Close was burning car tyres. The acrid smoke drifted sluggishly over a rooftop. Not one house in the Close had its full complement of windows. Fences were broken, or gone.

Gardens were full of rubbish, black plastic bags had been split by ravenous dogs, televisions flickered and blared. A police car drove into the Close and stopped. A policeman pulled a youth off the pavement, threw him into the back of the car and sped away with the youth struggling in the back. A man lay under a wreck of a car which was jacked up on bricks. Other men squatted close by, aiming torches and watching, men with outdated haircuts and tattoos, their cigarettes cupped in their hands. A woman in white stilettoes ran down the road after a boy toddler, naked apart from his vest. She yanked the child by his fat little arm back into the house.

'Now gerrin' and stay in,' she screamed. ''Oo left the bleedin' door open?' she demanded of other, unseen children.

The Queen was reminded of the stories that Crawfie would tell in the nursery at teatime. Of goblins and witches, of strange lands populated by sinister people. The Queen would beg her governess to stop, but she never would.

'Och awa' wi' you,' she'd laugh. 'You're far too soft.' Crawfie never spoke or laughed like that in Mama's presence.

The Queen thought, Crawfie knew. She knew. She was preparing me for Hell Close.

William and Harry ran up and down the Close, excited by the novelty of the journey, taking advantage of Nanny's absence. Ma and Pa were at the front door of a dirty old house, trying to get a key in the lock. William said, 'What are you doing, Pa?'

'Trying to get inside.'

'Why?'

'Because we're going to live here.'

William and Harry laughed loudly. It wasn't often Pa made a joke. He sometimes put on a silly voice and said things about the Goons and stuff, but mostly he was dead serious. Frowning and giving lectures.

Mama said, 'This is our new house.'

William said, 'How can it be new when it's old?'

Again the boys laughed. William lost control and needed support, he leaned against the creosoted fence dividing their house from its neighbour. The tired fence gave way under his fragile weight and collapsed. Seeing him there, fallen and shrieking amongst splintered wood, Diana automatically looked for Nanny, who always knew what to do, but Nanny wasn't there. She bent down and lifted her son from the wreckage. Harry whimpered and clung to the hem of her denim jacket. Charles booted furiously at the front door, which opened, releasing a stench of neglect and damp and ghostly chip fat. He switched on the hall light and beckoned his wife and children inside.

Tony Threadgold lit a cigarette and passed it to his wife. Then he lit one for himself. His good manners were often mocked at the Flowers Estate Working Men's Club. He had once said, 'Excuse me,' as he struggled through the scrum at the bar with a tray of drinks, only to have his sexuality challenged.

'"Excuse me?"' mocked a fat man with psychotic eyes. 'What are you, a poofter?'

Tony had brought the tray of drinks crashing down on the man's head: but then had immediately gone to

Bev and apologised for the delay in obtaining more drinks. Lovely manners.

The Threadgolds watched as a shadowy figure ordered a tall man out of the van. Was she a foreigner? It wasn't English she was talking was it? But as their ears became more accustomed they realised it was English, but posh English, *really* posh.

'Tone, why they moved a posho in Hell Close?' asked Beverley.

'Dunno,' replied Tony, peering into the gloom. 'Seen her somewhere before. Is she Dr Khan's receptionist?'

'No,' said Beverley (who was always at the doctor's, so she spoke with some authority), 'definitely not.'

'Christ, just our bleedin' luck to have poshos nex' door.'

'Least they won't shit in the bath, like the last lot of mongrels.'

'Yeah, there is that,' conceded Tony.

Prince Philip stared speechlessly at Number Nine. A street light flickered into life, casting a theatrical glow over his dilapidated future home. It continued to flicker as though it belonged in the theatre and was auditioning for a storm at sea. The driver let down the ramp at the back of the van and went inside. He'd never seen such lovely stuff – not in twenty-one years of removals. The dog in the cage at the back started to growl and snap and hurl its ferocious little body against the bars.

'They've got a dog,' said Tony.

'So long as they keep it under control,' said Beverley.

Tony squeezed his wife's shoulder. She was a good kid, he thought. Tolerant like.

Prince Philip spoke. 'It's abso-bloody-lutely impossible. I refuse. I'd sooner live in a bloody *ditch*. And that bloody *light* will send me *mad*.'

He shouted up at the light which carried on with its storm-at-sea impression, taking on hurricane status when Philip took hold of its post and shook it violently from side to side.

Beverley said, 'I got it. He's a loony, one of them that's been let out to die in the community.'

Tony watched as Philip ran to the back of the van and screamed at the little dog, 'Quiet, Harris! You sodding little turd!'

'You might be right, Bev,' said Tony. They turned to go back into their house when the Queen addressed them.

'Excuse me, but would you have an axe I could borrow?'

'An *ix*?' repeated Tony.

'Yes, an axe.' The Queen came to their front gate.

'An *ix*?' puzzled Beverley.

'Yes.'

'I dunno what an "ix" *is*,' Tony said.

'You don't know what an axe is?'

'No.'

'One uses it for chopping wood.'

The Queen was growing impatient. She had made a simple request; her new neighbours were obviously morons. She was aware that educational standards had fallen, but not to know what an *axe* was ... It was a scandal.

'I need an implement of some kind to gain access to my house.'

'Arse?'

'*House!*'

The driver volunteered his services as translator. His hours talking to the Queen had given him a new found linguistic confidence.

'This lady wants to know if you've got a *axe*.'

'Yeah, I got a axe, but I ain't 'anding it over to 'im,' said Tony, pointing at Philip. The Queen came down the garden path towards the Threadgolds and the light from their hall illuminated her face. Beverley gasped and curtsied clumsily. Tony reeled back and clutched the lintel of the front door for support before saying, 'It's out the back, I'll geddit.'

Left alone, Beverley burst into tears.

'It was the shock,' she said later, as she and Tony lay in bed unable to sleep.

'I mean, who would believe it? I still don't believe it, Tone.'

'Nor do I, Bev. I mean, the Queen next door. We'll put in for a transfer, eh?'

Slightly comforted, Beverley went to sleep.

It was Tony Threadgold who had prised the boards from the front door, but it was Prince Philip who had taken the key from his wife, turned it in the lock and entered the house. It was ludicrously small, of course.

'I had a wendy house bigger than this,' said the Queen, as she peered into the main living room.

'We've had bloody *cars* bigger than this,' said Prince

Philip as he stomped up the stairs. The whole interior was papered with anaglypta. It had been painted magnolia throughout. 'Very nice,' said the driver. 'Clean.'

Tony Threadgold said, 'Yeah, after the Smiths were chucked out, the council cleaning squad 'ad to come in. Wore protective clothing like, and those 'elmets what gives oxygen. Filthy bleeders the Smiths were. So you're lucky, you got it all done up, decorated.'

Beverley brought five mugs of strong tea round from next door. She gave the uncracked mug to the Queen. Prince Philip got the next best, the one with Alton Towers written on it. She gave herself the worst, the one with the slow leak which said, 'A BONK A DAY KEEPS THE DOCTOR AWAY'. The telephone rang, startling them all. Prince Philip located it inside the gas meter cupboard.

'It's for you,' he said, handing the receiver to his wife.

Jack Barker was on the line. 'How do you like it?' he said.

'I don't like it. Anyway, how do *you* like it, Mr Barker?'

'Like what?'

'Downing Street. It's an awful lot of work. All those red boxes.'

'Red boxes!' scoffed Barker. 'I've got better things to do than faff about with *them*. Goodnight.'

The Queen put the phone down and said, 'We'd better start bringing in the furniture, hadn't we?'

5 Kitchen Cabinet

At ten o'clock, Tony Threadgold plugged the Queen's television into the cracked wall socket and after jiggling about with the aerial socket, switched the set on.

'Uh, cowin' politics,' he said, as Jack Barker's face swam onto the screen.

Tony went to turn the set off, but the Queen said, 'No, please leave it on.' And she sat back to watch.

It was the first time that the kitchen of Number Ten Downing Street had been used in a Prime Ministerial Broadcast. Jack's new cabinet – six women, six men – sat around the large kitchen table, trying to look relaxed. Jack sat in a Windsor chair at the head of the table, facing the camera. Official-looking papers, coffee cups, a bowl of fruit and small vases of garden flowers had been artfully arranged by the director of the broadcast to suggest a business-like informality.

Jack's denim shirt sleeves were rolled to the elbow. His already handsome features had been further enhanced by subtle touches of colour. His accent combined the flattened vowels of the north with the crisper intonation of the south. He knew his smile was good, he used it often. He had alarmed his civil servants by telling them that he intended to write his own speeches and it was his own speech that he was reading now on the autocue. Even to his own ears it sounded stilted and ridiculous. But it was too late to change it now:

'Citizens! We are no longer subjects! Every man, woman and child in the land can raise their heads higher today, free at last of the pernicious class system that has poisoned our society for so long. From this day forward, all ranks, titles and positions of privilege are abolished. Citizens will be known only as Mr, Mrs, Ms or Miss.

'The parasitic Royal Family are to be relocated to an area where they will live ordinary lives amongst ordinary people. It will be a criminal offence to curtsey, bow, or to address them with other than the aforesaid forms of address. Their lands, properties, pictures, furniture, jewels, breeding stock, etc, etc, etc, belong, in their entirety, to the State. People wishing to ingratiate themselves with the former Royal Family are advised that such behaviour, should it come to the notice of the authorities, will be punished.

'However, the ex-Royal Family will be protected by the laws of the land. Anybody intimidating, threatening or abusing them, or causing them harm, or invading their privacy will be dealt with in the criminal courts. It is to be hoped that the members of the ex-Royal Family will integrate themselves into their local community, find employment and become useful members of society – something they have not been for many hundreds of years.

'The Crown Jewels are to be auctioned at Sotheby's as soon as arrangements are completed. The proceeds from this sale will go towards maintaining Britain's housing stock. The Japanese government has shown interest in this sale. It is not true that the Crown Jewels are "priceless". Everything has a price.

'So, fellow citizens, hold your head high. You are no longer subjugated.'

'Well, what did you think?' said Jack.

'You sounded a bit poncy,' said Pat Barker. They were sitting up in bed in Number Ten Downing Street. The bed was piled high with documents and draft proposals and official and personal letters. A fax machine spewed out information, congratulations and abuse. The click of the ansafone was a constant background noise. Jack had spoken to the American President five minutes previously. The President had assured Jack that he had 'never been comfortable with your monarchy, Jack'.

Despite himself, Jack had been thrilled to hear that familiar drawl. It was something he would have to watch in himself. He had a tendency to enjoy these contacts with famous people, but perhaps now that he was famous himself. . . .

Pat Barker offered her husband a cheese and potato crisp sandwich and said, 'What are you going to do about the pound, Jack?' Money had flooded out of the country as though a dam had burst.

'I'm going to meet the Japanese on Monday,' he said.

The Queen heaved herself off the packing case she had been sitting on to watch the broadcast. There was so much to do. She went to the hallway and saw Tony and Beverley dragging a double mattress up the narrow stairs. Philip followed behind, carrying a carved bedhead. He said,

'Lilibet, I can't find another bed in the van.' The Queen frowned and said,

'But I'm sure I asked for two beds, one for me and one for you.'

Philip said, 'So how are we supposed to *sleep* tonight?'

'Together,' she said.

6 Bisecting the Sofa

The carpets were too big for the tiny rooms.

Tony said, 'I've got a mate, Spiggy, what's a carpet fitter. He could cut 'em to size; he'd do it for twenty quid.'

The Queen looked down at her Aubusson rugs which were stacked in the hall, looking like lustrous Swiss rolls.

Bev said, 'Or you could have new. I mean, excuse me for saying, but they are a bit worn, aren't they? Threadbare in places.'

'Spiggy could carpet the whole house for two hundred and fifty quid, including fitting,' Tony suggested helpfully. 'He's got some nice olive green shag pile, we've got it in our living room.'

It was 10.30 pm and the furniture was still in the van. The driver was asleep with his head on the steering wheel.

'Philip?'

The Queen was tired – she had never been so tired. She couldn't make any decisions. She wanted to retire to her room in Buckingham Palace, where her nightgown would be laid out. She wanted to slide between the linen sheets and drop her head onto the soft pillows and sleep forever, or until somebody brought the tea tray in the morning. Philip

43

sat on the stairs, his head between his hands. He was exhausted after helping to carry the carpets in from the van. He had thought he was fit. Now he knew he wasn't.

'I don't bloody know. Do as you like,' he said.

'Send for Mr Spiggy,' said the Queen.

Spiggy turned up three-quarters of an hour later with his Stanley knife and his metal tape measure and his four tins of Carlsberg. The Queen was unable to watch while Spiggy sliced and chopped at her precious rugs. She took the dog for a walk, but when she got to the end of the Close she was turned back by polite policemen manning a hastily constructed barrier. An Inspector Denton Holyland emerged from a little hut and explained that the rest of the Flowers Estate was out of bounds to her and her family, 'until further notice'.

'I've already explained to your son,' he said. 'He wanted to find a fish and chip shop but I had to turn him back. Mr Barker's orders.'

The Queen walked around the Close four times. Nobody was about apart from the odd mongrel dog. She thought, I am living in a ghetto. I must consider myself a prisoner of war. I must be brave, I must maintain my own high standards. She knocked on her son's front door. 'May I come in?'

Diana was in the hall. The Queen could see she had been crying. It wouldn't do to sympathise, not now, thought the Queen.

'Our carpets won't fit,' gulped Diana, 'and the furniture is still in the van.'

Prince Charles and the driver of their removal van

came into sight, struggling with an unwieldy Chinese carpet.

'Not a hope, darling,' panted Prince Charles.

'Do be careful of your back, Charles,' said the Queen. 'There's a little man up the road who will cut carpets to size. . . .'

'Mummy, I really think that you er – shouldn't . . . isn't it frightfully patronising . . . I mean, in our present circumstances . . . to call anyone "a little man"?'

'But he *is* a little man,' said the Queen. 'Mr Spiggy is even smaller than I am and he's a carpet fitter. Shall I ask him to call?'

'But these carpets are *priceless*. It would be an act of er . . . well, sheer vandalism. . . .'

William and Harry appeared at the top of the stairs. They were dressed in pyjamas with Bart Simpson slippers on their feet.

'We're sleeping on a mattress,' piped Harry.

'In sleeping bags,' bragged William. 'Pa says we're having an adventure.'

Diana showed the Queen around the house. It didn't take long. The décor had been chosen by someone who had never heard of Terence Conran. Diana shuddered at the purple and turquoise wallpaper on the walls of the marital bedroom, the polystyrene ceiling tiles, the orange paintwork splodged over the sash window.

She thought, I'll ring *Interiors* tomorrow, ask the editor to come round with paint charts and wallpaper samples.

The Queen said, 'We're lucky, we've been decorated throughout.'

Both women were rather dreading the night to come. Neither was used to sharing either a bedroom or a bed with her husband.

The two little boys lay on their backs and gazed rapturously at their Superman wallpaper.

'And look,' said William, pointing to a round patch of mould above the window. 'That's the planet Krypton.'

But Harry had gone to sleep with one hand flopping off the mattress and onto the dirty bare boards of the bedroom floor.

Spiggy drank the last of his cans and surveyed his handiwork. The carpets glowed under the bare bulbs. The Queen gathered the offcuts together and put them in the box room – preparing for the day when they would be woven back and relaid in Buckingham Palace. Because this nonsense wouldn't last long. It was a hiccup of history. Mr Barker would make a dreadful hash of things and the populace would cry out for the restoration of the Conservative government and the monarchy – wouldn't they? Yes, of course they would. The English were known for their tolerance, their sense of fair play. Extremism of any kind was simply not in their nature. The Queen was careful, even in thought to distinguish the English from the Scots, Irish and Welsh, who, owing to their Celtic blood, were inclined to be rather hot-headed at times.

'That'll be fifty quid, Your Majesty,' said Spiggy. 'Being as it's after midnight, so to speak.'

The Queen found her handbag and paid him. She was unaccustomed to handling money and counted it out slowly.

'Right, ta,' said Spiggy. 'I'll nip round to Prince Charles's now. He'll still be up, will he?'

It was 4 am before Spiggy checked out at the barrier, a hundred pounds better off and with a story to tell in the pub the next day. He could hardly wait, his tongue itched.

At 4.30 am, Tony Threadgold was sawing through a sofa that had once belonged to Napoleon, on the doorstep of Number Nine. Nobody in Hell Close complained about the noise. Noise was normal and was created with great vigour, both day and night. It was only when there was a *lack* of noise that the inhabitants of Hell Close came to their doors and windows, wondering what was wrong.

The sofa gave way and fell apart. Beverley steadied one end. She waited until Tone and Philip had carried the longer half into the living room before following them through with the shorter half.

'Half a dozen six-inch nails in that tomorrow, it'll be as right as rain.' Tony was pleased with his carpentry. The Queen looked at her beloved sofa and saw that, even cut in half, it was too big for the room.

'You've been so kind, Mr and Mrs Threadgold,' she said. 'Now I *insist* you go to your beds.'

'It does look lovely in here,' said Bev, looking round. 'A bit crowded, but lovely.'

'When the pictures are hung,' said the Queen, yawning.

'Yes, I like that one,' said Bev, catching the yawn. 'Who did that one?'

'Titian,' said the Queen. 'Goodnight.'

The atmosphere between the Queen and Prince Philip was awkward as they washed and undressed for bed. Furniture filled every room. They had to squeeze past each other with frequent apologies for touching. Finally, they lay in bed in the grey light of morning, thinking about the horrors of the previous day and of the horrors to come.

From outside came the sound of shouting as a milkman tried to defend his float from a Hell Close milk thief. The Queen turned towards her husband. He was still a handsome man, she thought.

7 Little Treasures

The Yeoman of the Silver Plate scrutinised Jack Barker, the new Prime Minister.

Very nice, he thought. Smaller than he looked on the telly, but very *nice*. Clothes a bit Top Man and shoes a touch Freeman Hardyish, but a good, fine-boned face, *adorable* eyes – violet, and lashes like spiders' legs. Yum yum.

It was 9 am. They were going down in the lift of the disused air-raid shelter which was situated in the grounds of Buckingham Palace. Jack stifled a yawn. He'd been up all night doing his sums. 'I expect you're glad to get out of those daft clothes at night, aren't you?' he said to the Yeoman, looking at the gaiters and buckles and the jacket with its complicated froggings and fastenings.

'Oh, I like a bit of glitz, me,' said the Yeoman, producing a key from his waistcoat pocket. The lift stopped.

'How deep are we?' asked Jack.

'Forty feet, but we're not there yet.'

They left the lift and walked along a U-shaped corridor.

'What's your name?' asked Jack.

'Officially I'm the Yeoman of the Silver Plate.'

'Unofficially?' said Jack.

'Malcolm Bultitude Bostock.'

'Worked here long, Mr Bostock?'

'Since leaving school, Mr Barker.'

'Like it?'

'Oh yes, I like nice things. I miss the daylight in the summer, but I've got a sun-bed at home.'

They came up to the fourteen-inch thick steel door which was protected by an intricate combination lock. Mr Bostock inserted the key and after a series of clicks the door swung open. 'Just a mo,' he said, and switched the lights on. They were in an area the size of a football pitch which was divided into a series of doorless rooms. Each room was lined with shelves covered in industrial plastic sheeting.

Mr Bostock asked, 'Anything in particular you want to see, Mr Barker?'

'Everything,' said Jack.

'Most of the collection's at Sandringham, of course,' said Bostock, pulling the sheeting away and revealing an array of exquisitely carved animals. Jack picked up a jewelled cat.

'Pretty.'

'Fabergé.'

'How much do you reckon they're worth?' asked Jack, indicating the twinkling menagerie.

'Oh, I couldn't possibly say, Mr Barker,' said Mr Bostock, replacing the cat.

'Guess.'

'Well, something in the paper *did* catch my eye last year. A Fabergé tortoise it was, fetched £250,000 at auction.'

Jack looked again at the little animals. He counted them under his breath.

Mr Bostock said. 'There are four hundred and eleven of them.'

'Enough to build a hospital,' Jack muttered.

'*Several* hospitals,' corrected Mr Bostock, huffily.

They moved on. Jack was amazed at the insouciant manner in which the treasure was stored and displayed.

'Oh dear, we could do with a bit of a tidy up here,' said Mr Bostock, scooping up a few emeralds that had escaped from their plastic box. 'Takes four strong men to lift that,' he said, pointing out a massive silver soup tureen. And, further on, 'Gold is a bugger to clean,' as he parted the plastic sheeting to reveal a tower of gold plates, bowls and serving dishes.

Jack whispered, '*Real* gold?'

'Eighteen carat.'

Jack remembered that his wife's fourteen carat wedding ring had cost him £115 ten years ago and *that* had a hole in it.

'Does anybody come down here?' he asked Mr Bostock.

'She comes, about twice a year, but it's more of a personnel exercise, if you get my drift. She doesn't *gloat*. The last time she was here, she asked if the temperature couldn't be turned down; she doesn't like wasting money.'

'No, well, I can see how she'd have to be careful,' said Jack as he fingered a scabbard presented to Queen Victoria by an Arabian prince. He had given up asking the value of the treasures. The figures became meaningless and Mr Bostock was clearly uncomfortable talking about money.

'So, this is only a part of the collection, is it?' Jack

asked when they had visited each wondrous room.

'Tip of the iceberg.'

As they ascended in the lift, back to the daylight and the birdsong and the murmur of traffic, Jack thanked Mr Bostock and said, 'There'll be some foreign gentlemen to show round later this week. I'll be in touch directly.'

'Might I ask what type of foreign gentlemen?' said Mr Bostock, tilting his face towards the sun.

'Japanese,' said Jack Barker.

'And might I ask if I'm to keep my present position, Mr Barker?'

Jack repeated one of his election slogans: 'In Barker's Britain everything and everyone will work.'

They crossed the dew-covered lawn together, discussing Japanese protocol and precisely how low the Yeoman of the Silver Plate should bow when he greeted the visitors who came, not bearing gifts, but buying them.

8 Client Resistant

The cold woke her and she was enveloped in misery before her strength and resources could be summoned. Harris scrabbled at the bedroom door, desperate to get out. The Queen put a cashmere cardigan on over her nightdress, went downstairs and let the dog out into the back garden. The April air was raw and as she watched him lift his leg in the frosty grass, her breath puffed out, white and visible in front of her. A heap of empty Magnolia paint tins lay in the garden. Somebody had tried to set fire to them, lost heart and left them. The Queen called the little dog inside, but he wanted to explore this new territory and ran on his ridiculous little legs to the end of the garden, where he disappeared into the mist.

When Harris reappeared he was carrying a dead rat in his mouth. The rat was frozen into an attitude of extreme agony. It took a sharp crack on the head with a wooden spoon before Harris would release his gift to the Queen. She had once eaten a mouthful of rat at a banquet in Belize. To have refused would have caused great offence. The RAF were anxious to retain the use of Belize as a refuelling stop.

'Mornin'. Sleep all right?'

It was Beverley in an orange dressing gown taking frozen washing off the line. Tony's jeans stood to attention as though Tony were still inside them. "E's got an interview for a job 's afternoon, so I've gotta get 'is best clothes dry.'

Beverley's heart pounded as she spoke. How did you talk to someone whose head you were used to licking and sticking on an envelope? She unpegged Tony's best jumper which was frozen into an attitude of arms-raised triumph.

'Harris found a rat,' said the Queen.

'A ret?'

'A *rat*, look!' Beverley looked down at the dead rodent at the Queen's feet. 'Am I to expect more?'

'Don't worry,' said Beverley. 'They don't come in the houses. Well, not often. They've got their own complex at the bottom of the gardens.'

Beverley made it sound as though the rats inhabited a timeshare village, frolicked in a kidney-shaped swimming pool and argued over sun-loungers.

Somebody was knocking on the front door. The Queen excused herself and went through the little hall. She put a coat on over her nightdress and cardigan and tried to open the door. It was extraordinarily difficult. True, it was years since she'd opened the front door of any house, but surely it had been easier than this? She pulled with all her weight. Meanwhile, the person on the other side of the door had opened the letter-box. The Queen saw a pair of soulful brown eyes and heard a sympathetic female voice.

'Hi, I'm Trish McPherson. I'm your social worker. Look, I know it's difficult for you, but it's not going to help the situation if you won't let me in, is it?'

The Queen recoiled from the words 'social worker' and stepped back from the door. Trish remembered her training; it was important to be non-confrontational. She tried again, 'C'mon now, Mrs Windsor, open the door and we'll have a nice chat. I'm here to help you with your trauma. We'll put the kettle on and have a nice cup of tea, shall we?'

The Queen said, 'I am not dressed. I cannot receive visitors until I am dressed.'

Trish laughed gaily, 'Don't worry about me; I take folks as I find them. Most of my clients are still in bed when I call.'

Trish knew that she was a good person and she was convinced that most of her clients were good, deep down. She felt truly sorry for the Queen. Her fellow social workers had refused to take on the Windsor case file but, as Trish had said in the intake office this morning, 'They may be royal, but they are human. To me, they are just two displaced pensioners who will need a great deal of support.'

Not wishing to antagonise her client, Trish withdrew, wrote a note on Social Services notepaper and pushed it through the door. It said, 'I will call round this afternoon, about three. Yours, Trish.'

The Queen went upstairs, scraped the ice from the inside of the window and looked down at Trish, who was scraping ice off the windscreen of her car with what looked like a kitchen spatula, the sort the Queen occasionally used at barbecues at Balmoral. Trish was dressed in Aztec-styled clothes and could easily have strayed off the stage during a performance of *The Royal Hunt of the Sun*. She appeared to be wearing parts of a dead goat on her feet. She sat in the car and made notes, 'Client resistant; not dressed at 10 am.'

When the Queen heard the car draw away she went to her husband, who was lying on his back in a deep sleep. A dewdrop hung from his craggy nose. The Queen took a handkerchief from her handbag and wiped the dewdrop away. She didn't know how to continue with her day: bathing, dressing and doing her own hair seemed to be insurmountable problems. I couldn't even open my own front *door*, she thought. The only thing she was certain of was that she wouldn't be at home to visitors at 3 pm.

There was no hot water in the icy bathroom, so she washed in cold. Her hair was impossible; it had lost its set. She did the best she could and eventually tied a scarf, gypsy-fashion, around her head. How very awkward it was to dress oneself, how fiddly buttons were! Why did zips stick so? How on earth did one choose what went with what? She thought of the corridors lined with closets where her clothes used to hang in colour co-ordinated rows. She missed the deft fingers of her dresser fastening her brassière. What a ludicrous device a brassière was! How did other women cope with those hooks and eyes? One needed to be a contortionist to bring the two together without assistance.

When the Queen was dressed, she had a terrific sense of achievement. She wanted to tell somebody, like the day she had tied her shoelaces for the first time. Crawfie had been so pleased. 'Guid girrl. You'll never have to do it for yourself, of course, but it's as well to know – much like logarithms.'

The only source of heat in the house was the gas fire in the living room. Beverley had turned it on last night, but now the Queen was baffled. She turned the knob to full, held a match to the ceramic element, but nothing happened. She was anxious to have at least one warm room before Philip woke and (perhaps she was being over-ambitious) she planned to make breakfast: tea and toast. She imagined Philip and herself sitting by the gas fire planning their new lives. She had always had to placate Philip, he had resented walking one step behind her. His personality was not in tune with playing second fiddle. He was a whole quarreling orchestra.

Harris came in as she was holding the last match to the recalcitrant gas fire. He was hungry and cold and there was nobody to give him food, apart from herself. She was torn between the fire and Harris. There is so much to *do*, thought the Queen. So many tasks. How do ordinary people *manage*?

'The secret is one puts a fifty pence piece in the slot,' said Prince Charles. He had gained access to his mother's house by knocking on the living room window and climbing through. He opened the meter cupboard and showed his mother the metal slot.

'But I haven't got a fifty pence piece,' said the Queen.

'Neither have I. Would Papa have one?'

'Why would Papa have one?'

'Quite. William may have one in his piggy bank. Should I . . . er . . . go and. . . ?'

'Yes, tell him I'll pay him back.'

The Queen was struck by the change in her son.

He started to climb out of the front window, then came back for a moment.

'Mama?'

'Yes, darling?'

'A social worker called on us this morning.'

'Trish McPherson?'

'Yes. She was awfully nice. She told me that I could have my ears fixed on the National Health. She told me that I have been damaged psychologically ... er ... and I think she's ... well ... sort of, er ... right. Diana's thinking about having her nose done. She's always hated it.' As Charles bounded past her living room window, the Queen thought: how happy he looks on what should be the most miserable day of his life!

Upstairs, Prince Philip stirred. There was something disagreeable on the end of his nose. He said, 'Fetch me a handkerchief, quickly!' to a non-existent servant. After a few seconds, he remembered where he was. Looking around helplessly, he capitulated to his present circumstances and wiped his nose himself on the bed sheet. He then turned over and went back to sleep; preferring royal dreamland to the hideous reality of being a commoner in a cold house.

The Queen unpacked the cardboard box stamped 'FOOD'. In it she found a loaf of bread labelled 'THICK SLICED MOTHER'S PRIDE', a half pound of Anchor butter, a jar of strawberry jam, a tin of corned beef, a tin of Heinz tomato soup, a tin of stewed steak, a tin of new potatoes, a tin of marrowfat peas, a tin of peaches (sliced) in syrup, a packet of digestive biscuits, a packet of Mr Kipling jam tarts, a jar of Nescafé, a packet of Typhoo tea bags, a box of Long-Life milk, a bag of white sugar, a small box of cornflakes, a packet of salt, a bottle of HP sauce, a Birds Eye trifle kit, a packet of Kraft cheese slices, and six eggs (presumably laid by the battery method since there was nothing on the box boasting that the chickens led a healthy outdoor life).

Harris eyed the tins greedily, but the Queen said, 'Nothing for you, old boy.' She picked up the tin of corned beef. It looks quite like dog food, she thought, but how does one gain access to it?

She read the instructions: 'Use key,' it said. She located the key which was flattened against the tin like a sentry in a box. But now, having found it, what did one *do* with it? Harris barked irritably as he watched the Queen fumbling with the corned beef tin: trying to fit the key into a raised metal strip at the base. The Queen said, 'Please Harris, do be patient, I'm doing my best: I'm hungry and cold and you're not helping me at all.' And she thought (but did not say aloud), and my husband is upstairs in bed and *he*'s not helping me either.

She turned the key and Harris leaped towards the tin as the stale blood smell of the corned beef was released into the air. He barked frantically and even the Queen, whose tolerance of noisy barking was legendary, lost her temper and slapped Harris's nose. Harris retreated glowering under the sink. After a long struggle the Queen removed the base of the tin. The speckled pink block was clearly seen but however hard she shook the tin it refused to move. Perhaps if she tried to grasp the meat with her fingers. . . ?

When Charles returned through the window, proudly holding the fifty pence piece aloft as though it were a trophy, he found his mother leaning against a semi-circular William Gates cabinet, which now served as a hall table. A pool of blood gathered on the exquisite surface. Harris was under the cabinet attacking a tin and issuing primeval guttural growls. From upstairs came the fearful sound of his father in a rage. Charles had been taught how to cope with his paternal terror by a Gestalt therapist, so he blocked out his father's obscenities by dating the William Gates cabinet.

'1781,' he said. 'Built for George IV.'

'Yes, very clever, darling, but I rather think I may be bleeding to death. Would you ask my doctor to attend to me?'

The Queen took the scarf from around her head and bound it around her bleeding fingers. Philip came to the top of the stairs, shivering in a silk dressing gown.

They waited four and a half hours before the Queen was seen by a doctor at the Royal Hospital. There was fog on the motorway and road hogs and their victims cluttered the casualty department of the Royal Hospital.

Charles, the Queen and an armed, but plain-clothed, policeman had driven past the barrier at the end of Hell Close just as Princess Margaret's pantechnicon had driven in. Princess Margaret had looked down into the police car and seen her sister's blood-stained cash-mere jumper and her closed eyes and had immediately had hysterics, shrieking, 'They are going to kill us all!'

The driver of the pantechnicon had turned murder-ous eyes onto her. After enduring three hours of her company he could cheerfully have put her up against a wall, a scarf around her eyes, a bullet in her heart. He would have denied her a last cigarette.

All through the afternoon, Charles and his mother sat behind a thin curtain in a cubicle at the Royal Hospital, listening to the almost unbearable sounds of human suffering. They heard death, agony and the desperate laughter of teenage nurses as they tried to remove a withered rubber doll from the penis of a middle-aged man. The Queen almost laughed herself when she heard the man's wife say to the nurses, 'I *knew* there was someone else.'

But she didn't laugh. She pulled her features into a scowl. Crawfie had taught her to control her emotions, and the Queen was grateful for Crawfie's wise guidance. How else could she have borne all those interminable speeches of welcome, in languages she didn't understand, knowing that she must sit through the translation into English. Then to have to rise and read out her own banalities, and then to inspect the troops, knowing that each man or woman dreaded her stopping at *them*. And what did she say when she did stop? 'Where are you from? How long have you been in the Army?' It was painful to watch them stammering a reply. Once she had asked, 'Do you like the Navy?' of a young sailor of eighteen. He had instantly replied,

'No, Your Majesty.' She had scowled and moved on. But she had wanted to smile and thank him for his rare honesty. She had given instructions that he was not to be punished.

'I am sorry to keep you, Mrs Windsor. I'm Doctor Animba.' The doctor had been warned, but he felt his blood pressure rise as he took the Queen's injured hand in his own. Tenderly he removed the bloodstained dressing and inspected the deep cuts on the thumb and two fingers.

'And how did you do this, Your Maj – . . . Mrs Windsor?'

'On a corned beef tin.'

'A very common injury. Legislation is called for. Those tins should be outlawed.'

Doctor Animba was a serious young man who believed that the law could cure most social ills.

Charles said, 'Dr Animba, my mother has waited nearly *five hours* for medical attention.'

'Yes, this is normal.' Doctor Animba rose to his feet.

'Normal?'

'Oh yes. Your mother is lucky she did not choose to eat corned beef on a Saturday night. On Saturday nights we are extremely busy. Now I must go. A nurse will be coming along soon.' With a swish of the curtain he was gone. The Queen sank back onto the hospital trolley and closed her eyes tightly against the prickling of tears gathering behind the lids. She *must* control herself at all costs.

Charles said, 'It's another world.'

The Queen said, 'Another country, at least.'

They heard Doctor Animba go into the cubicle containing the rubber doll and her victim. They heard his vigorous struggle as he endeavoured to part rubber from flesh. They heard him say, 'There should be legislation.'

Red with embarrassment, Charles said, 'I was supposed to be opening a new hospital in Taunton tomorrow.'

The Queen said, 'I expect the populace of Taunton will cope with your absence.'

They waited in silence for the promised nurse. Eventually, the Queen fell asleep. Prince Charles looked at his mother, her untidy hair, her bloodstained jumper. He took her uninjured hand in his hand and vowed to take care of her.

9 Faux Pas

That afternoon, Diana's tiny living room was full of visitors, all women. Some of them had brought autograph books. The room reeked of Christmas present perfume. Perfume that had been manufactured in industrial units in the Far East. Violet Toby, one of Diana's next-door neighbours, was telling Diana the story of her long life. The other women fidgeted, lit cigarettes, tugged on their skirts. They had heard this story many times before.

'So, when I seen this letter, I *knew*. So when he came home from work I said to 'im, who's this bleedin' *Yvonne* when she's at home? Well, 'is face went white. I said, You can gerrout and stay out. So that was number two.'

Diana prompted, as she had been taught to do, 'And did you marry again?'

Violet, who hadn't needed prompting, laughed. 'I'm on my fifth.'

All the women in the room laughed.

'Five husbands. Eleven children, fifteen grandchildren, six great-grandchildren, and there's a bloke at the British Legion I've set me cap at.' Violet applied scarlet lipstick to her mouth using the mirror on the inside of her plastic snakeskin handbag.

'You're a dirty bugger, Violet,' said Mandy Carter,

Diana's other next-door neighbour, whose fence Prince William had brought down the night before. Mandy nursed her new baby, called Shadow, on her shoulder. Diana looked at Mandy's clothes and barely suppressed a shudder. Stretch denim jeans with white stilettoes – ugh. And that blonde candy-floss hair with more split ends than a Chinese spring onion – gross. And those pale breasts spilling from that pink acrylic scooped neck top – mega vulgaris.

'Your 'usband and 'is mam 'ave bin a long time,' said Violet.

'Ya,' said Diana. 'Is the hospital far away?'

'Two mile down the road,' said a young woman with a spider tattooed on her neck.

'I were there six 'n 'alf hours that time Clive broke me jaw,' said Mandy.

'Gracious,' said Diana. 'Who's Clive?'

''Is dad,' said Mandy, darkly, pointing to Shadow. 'I cun't eat, cun't smoke, cun't drink.'

'Din't stop yer shagging though, did it?' said Violet. 'I 'eard you – and I'm two doors away.'

Diana blushed. Gracious, she was no prude, but she hated to hear a woman swear. She looked up just as Inspector Holyland passed by the dripping privet hedge. He glowered into the crowded living room. The women catcalled and the tattooed woman whistled, as though calling a taxi in London.

Holyland marched down the path. Diana picked her way through the women and answered her front door. Inspector Holyland coughed to give himself time. He had forgotten what he was supposed to call her. Was it Mrs Windsor? Mrs Spencer? Mrs Charles?

Diana waited until the policeman had recovered from his coughing fit. Eventually he spluttered, 'They shouldn't be in there,' pointing to the women in the living room. 'You're not supposed to receive any special attention.' He had got a grip on himself now. 'So I'd be obliged if you'd ask them to go, madam.'

'I couldn't possibly. It would be so rude.'

A cheer came from the living room and Violet bustled to the front door, hands in the pockets of her satin bomber jacket, an imperious expression on her wrinkled face. 'We ain't payin' her any special attention; we're 'er neighbours. We've come to see if she needs owt doin'.'

'Oh yes,' sneered Holyland. 'Do the same for *anybody*, do you?'

''S matter of fact, yes, we do,' said Violet, truthfully. 'We stick together in Hell Close.'

She turned to Diana. 'Right, shall we start on them cupboards?'

Holyland turned away. The records showed that Violet, her husband Wilf and seven of their adult children had not yet paid this year's poll tax – in fact, they had not yet paid *last* year's poll tax. He would get his revenge.

Just then, Diana saw the shape of Princess Margaret running down the middle of the road, high heels clacking, fur coat flying, hair escaping from its elaborate top knot. She ran up to the barrier and began to grapple with a young policeman. Inspector Holyland spoke into his radio and seconds later a klaxon sounded and the street was suddenly illuminated by harsh white light.

'Christ!' said Violet. 'It's like bleedin' Colditz.'

'It's Margo trying to break the seven o'clock curfew,' said Diana, watching from her doorstep. It was Inspector Holyland himself who escorted Princess Margaret back to her house.

Diana heard her say, 'But I *must* get to Marks and Spencer before they close. I can't cook.'

Diana shut her front door and went back to her neighbours. She looked forward to putting on an apron, getting into the kitchen and rattlin' those pots and pans, just like Little Richard ordered. She would borrow Violet's chip-pan tonight and cook egg, chips and beans for the family. Charles would have to compromise his dietary rules until she could organise a supply of pulses. She doubted if Violet had a jar of lentils she could borrow.

As they worked, Mandy asked, 'What will you miss most?'

Diana answered instantly, 'My Merc.'

'Merc?'

'Mercedes-Benz 500 SL. It's metallic red and it does one-hundred-and-fifty-seven miles an hour.'

'Bet that cost a bit,' said Mandy.

'Well, about seventy thousand pounds,' confessed Diana. The room went quiet.

'An' who paid for that?'

'The Duchy of Cornwall,' said Diana.

'Who's that?' asked Mandy.

'My husband, actually,' said Diana.

'Did you say *seventeen* thousand?' said Violet as she adjusted her pink hearing aid.

'*Seventy* thousand,' bellowed Philomena Toussaint, the only black woman in the room. There was silence.

67

'For a car?' Violet's chins wobbled in indignation. Diana dropped her eyes. She didn't yet know that the women cleaning her kitchen, whose clothes she despised, had bought those clothes in charity shops. Violet's 38 DD bra had been bought for twenty-five pence at Help the Aged.

Mandy broke the silence by saying, 'I'd miss the bleedin' nanny.'

This reminded Diana that she hadn't seen William or Harry since her visitors had arrived. She called upstairs but there was no answer. She looked outside into the sad-looking back garden, but the only sign of life was Harris ingratiating himself with a cross-breed alsatian belonging to Mandy Carter. The two dogs circled each other. The little and the large, the commoner and the aristocrat. The alsatian was called 'King'. Diana ran outside, calling, 'William, Harry.' It was nearly dark. Bare bulbs showed as Hell Close prepared for night.

'The boys have never been out in the dark before,' said Diana. The women laughed at this new evidence of the boys' pampered existence. They regularly sent their small children to the Indian shop for late night groceries. Why keep a dog and bark yourself?

'They'll be playing somewhere,' comforted Violet. But Diana would not be placated. Throwing on a silk parka, she strode out in her cowboy boots to search Hell Close. She finally located them playing battle-ships in front of the gas fire with their grandfather at Number Nine. She watched through the window until Harry saw her and waved. Prince Philip was wearing pyjamas and a dressing gown. He hadn't shaved and his hair hung over his ears in sparse strands. A tin of baked beans with a jagged open lid stood on the William III silver table.

'Charles telephoned,' Philip shouted through the window. 'They're still at the hospital. Can't ask you in; bloody front door won't open. Bloody back door key's lost.'

Diana took the hint and went back to her domestic tasks. When the kitchen cupboards had been thoroughly cleaned out, the women broke for tea and Silk Cuts.

'That should keep them at bay for a bit,' said Violet.

'Keep *what* at bay?' asked Diana.

'The cockroaches. We've all got 'em. Nothin' gets rid of 'em. You could fire a Polaris missile at 'em an' the buggers'd still come back three days later. Violet shifted gear. 'Right, what you need now is linin' paper, before you put your food in.'

Diana had nothing suitable, so Violet banged on the wall which divided her living room wall from Diana's and shouted, 'Wilf! Bring yesterday's paper round.'

Diana heard a muffled reply and soon Wilf Toby stood at the front door. He was an unusually tall man with powerful shoulders and huge feet and hands. The sort of man who is described in court as 'a gentle giant' by defence barristers. But Wilf Toby was not a gentle man. He had chronic bronchitis and his constant fight for breath made him irritable and morose. He feared death and lived each day timidly, as though it was to be his last. He felt that Violet ought to pay him more attention. He thought, she spends more time in other folk's houses than she does in her own. Hearing Wilf's ragged breath comforted Diana, for she now knew what the strange noise was that had kept her awake and terrified last night. It was Wilf, breathing next to the party wall.

Wilf looked at Diana and it was love at first sight. He'd never seen such a beautiful woman up close, in the flesh. He'd seen her photograph in the paper every day, but nothing had prepared him for the fresh face, the soft skin, the shy blue eyes, the warm damp lips. All the women Wilf knew had hard, rough-looking faces, as though life had battered them mercilessly. As Diana took the newspaper from him, he looked at her hands. Pale, long fingers with rosy nails. Wilf longed to hold those fingers. Would they feel as smooth as they looked?

He scrutinized Violet, his wife of four years. How had he ended up with *her*? But he knew how. She had hunted him down. He hadn't stood a chance.

'Well, come in or go out, you great big gorm face. You're letting the cold in.' Listen to how his wife spoke to him. No respect.

Diana smiled and said, 'Please come in.' Normally, nothing would have induced Wilf to leave the doorstep and enter a house full of Hell Close women, but he had to see Diana, listen to her lovely voice. She spoke beautiful, she really did.

The presence of a man in the house subdued the women. Even Violet modulated her voice as she folded pages of *The News of the World* and lined cupboards and drawers. Diana saw flashes of headlines.

POUND 'SAVAGED'

The pound was said to be in a critical condition last night after suffering what one financial expert described as 'a brutal attack' by foreign currency dealers. 'It was a savage beating,' he said.

This followed the 'double whammy' of Jack Barker's landslide victory at the polls on Thursday and the abolition of the monarchy on Friday. The Governor of the Bank of England has appealed for a period of calm.

Piranhas

A representative of the London office of the Bank of Tokyo said yesterday: 'The pound is a goldfish swimming in a tank of piranhas.'

When she had finished, Violet surveyed her work proudly. 'There, now; it's all nice and clean,' she said. Then, turning to Wilf, she snapped, 'I suppose you want your tea?'

'I'm not 'ungry,' said Wilf. How could he ever eat again? Diana longed for them all to go, but couldn't think how to make this known to them. Then Shadow woke from his temporary sleeping place on the velvet sofa and his screams drove his mother and the other women from the house.

'Knock on the wall if you want owt,' ordered Violet.

'Night or day,' added Wilf.

'You've been terribly kind,' said Diana. 'What do I owe you?' She opened her purse and looked inside. When she looked up, she saw from the expression on the women's faces that she had committed a major *faux pas*.

When Charles and Elizabeth arrived back at Number Nine, they found that Tony Threadgold had booted the front door open and was planing down the edge.

'Damp's warped it,' he explained. ''S why it wouldn't open.'

Prince Philip, William and Harry were sitting on the stairs watching Tony. All three were eating untidy jam sandwiches, prepared by William.

'How are you, old girl?' said Philip.

'Frightfully tired.' The Queen pushed her untidy hair back with the bandaged hand.

'Been a bloody long time,' her husband said.

'They were awfully busy,' explained Charles. 'Mummy's injury wasn't life threatening, so we had to wait.'

'But God damn it, your mother's the bloody *Queen*,' exploded Philip.

'*Was* the bloody Queen, Philip,' said the Queen quietly. 'I am now Mrs Windsor.'

'Mountbatten,' corrected Prince Philip tersely. 'You are now Mrs Mountbatten.'

'Windsor is *my* family name, Philip, and I intend to keep it.'

'Mountbatten is my family name, and you are my wife, therefore you are Mrs Mountbatten.'

Tony Threadgold planed away like a madman. They had obviously forgotten he was there. William asked Charles, 'What is *our* name now, Papa?'

Charles looked from one parent to the other. 'Er, Diana and I haven't discussed it yet . . . er . . . on the one hand, one feels drawn to Mountbatten because of Uncle Dickie, but on the other, one also feels, er . . . well . . . er. . . .'

'Oh, for Christ's sake!' Philip had turned nasty. 'Spit it out, boy.'

Tony thought it was time the Queen sat down; she was looking knackered. He took her arm and escorted her into the living room. The gas fire was out so he rummaged in his pocket, found a fifty pence piece and put it in the meter. The flames popped alive and the Queen leaned gratefully toward the heat.

'I think yer mam'd like a cup of tea,' prompted Tony to Charles. Tony had already realised that Philip was hopeless domestically, the man couldn't even dress himself. But when, after fifteen minutes during which Tony swept up the wooden shavings and smoothed down the edge of the door with sandpaper, Charles was *still* blundering about in the kitchen in a futile search for tea, milk and sugar spoons, Tony went next door and asked Bev to put the kettle on.

The Queen stared into the gas flames. She had thought that this Windsor/Mountbatten conflict had been laid to rest long ago, but now it had reared its ugly head again. It was Louis Mountbatten's fault. That odious snob had persuaded the Bishop of Carlisle to comment, on the occasion of Charlie's birth, that he did not like to think of a child born in wedlock being deprived of its father's name. The obscure cleric's comments had made national headlines. Louis Mountbatten's campaign to glorify his family name and make it that of the reigning house had started in earnest. The Queen had been torn between her husband's and Louis Mountbatten's wishes and those of King George V, who had founded the House of Windsor in perpetuity. The Queen closed her eyes. Louis was long gone, but he was still influencing events.

Beverley came in with a tray on which stood four steaming mugs of tea and two glasses of bright orange pop. Thick striped drinking straws bobbed about in the lurid liquid. A doyley-covered plate held an assortment of biscuits. Charles took the tray from Beverley, then hovered around looking for somewhere to place it. The Queen watched her son in growing irritation.

'On my desk, Charles!'

Charles placed the tray on the Chippendale desk, which stood in the window. He handed out the cups and glasses. He felt shy in Beverley's presence. Her fleshiness disturbed him. For a split second he saw her naked, draped in gauze, gazing at her own reflection in a mirror held by a cherub. A Venus of the 1990s. The Queen introduced them: 'This is Mrs Beverley Threadgold, Charles.'

'How do you do,' said Charles, offering his hand.

'I'm all right, thanks,' said Beverley, taking his hand and shaking it vigorously.

'My son, Charles Windsor,' said the Queen.

'Mountbatten,' corrected Philip. To Beverley he said, 'His name is Charles Mountbatten. I'm his father and he'll take my name.'

Charles thought it was high time to bring an end to this dreadful paternalism. What was the maiden name of Queen Mary, his great grandmother? Teck. Yes, that was it. How did 'Charlie Teck' sound?

'We will discuss this later, Philip,' the Queen warned.

'There is nothing to discuss. I'm the head of the household. I've had forty years of walking behind you. It's my turn to walk in front.'

'You want to run the household, Philip?'

'Yes, I do.'

'Then,' said the Queen, 'you had better go into the kitchen and familiarise yourself with the various implements and procedures needed for making tea. We cannot rely on Mrs Threadgold's generosity for ever.'

Beverley said, 'I'll give you lessons on making tea if you like. It's dead easy, really.'

But Prince Philip ignored her kind offer. Instead, he turned to Tony and complained, 'Can't get the hot water on; need a shave. See to it, will you?'

Tony bristled. Honest, he thought, he talks to me as if I'm a cowin' dog. 'Sorry,' he said, 'I'm taking Bev out for a drink. Ready, Bev?'

Beverley was pleased to have an excuse to start extricating herself from the site of so much marital tension.

Tony went home, taking his tool box with him. It had been a crap day all round. He hadn't got the job as a Halal chicken slaughterer – there had been a hundred and forty-four applicants in front of him, men and women of all religions. Beverley stayed on for a while and showed Prince Philip how to heat a saucepan of shaving water on the stove. She explained that the handle of the pan should be pointed away from the front of the stove. 'So the kids don't knock it.'

Charles came into the kitchen and watched gravely as though he were watching a demonstration of a Maori war dance. His two sons, their mouths stained orange, crept up and held his hands. They couldn't remember when they had seen so much of their father. When the water started to bubble, Beverley demonstrated how to turn the stove off. 'So what do I do now? said

Philip, plaintively. Beverley thought, well, I'm not bleedin' shavin' yer. She left the ex-Royal household gratefully.

'Like babies,' she said to Tony, as she changed into her going-to-the-pub clothes. ''S a wonder they can wipe their own bums.'

10 Keeping Warm

Next morning the frost was even heavier.

'You haven't shaved, Philip and it's nine o'clock.'

'I'm growing a beard.'

'You haven't washed.'

'Bathroom's bloody cold.'

'You've been wearing your pyjamas and dressing gown for two days.'

'Don't intend to go out. Why bother?'

'But you must go out.'

'Why?'

'For fresh air, exercise.'

'There is no fresh air in Hell bloody Close. It stinks. It's ugly. I refuse to acknowledge its existence. I shall stay in-bloody-doors until I die.'

'Doing what?'

'Nothing. Lying in bed. Now, leave my breakfast tray and close those bloody curtains and go out, would you?'

'Philip, you are talking to me as one would talk to a servant.'

'I'm your husband. You're my wife.'

Philip started to eat his breakfast. Boiled eggs, toast and coffee. The Queen closed the curtains, shutting out Hell Close, and went downstairs to call Harris in. She was worried about Harris. He had started to hang

77

around with a rough crowd. A pack of disreputable-looking mongrels, belonging to nobody in particular, it seemed, had started to gather in the Queen's front garden. Harris did nothing to discourage them, indeed he seemed to positively welcome their marauding presence.

Philomena Toussaint was awakened by the arrival of the Queen Mother moving into the pensioner's bungalow next door to her own. She got out of bed and put on the warm dressing gown that Fitzroy, her eldest son, had bought her for her eightieth birthday.

'Keep your bones warm, woman,' he had said, sternly. 'Wear the damn thing.'

She had read that the Queen Mother drank and gambled. Philomena disapproved of both. She offered a prayer to God. 'Lord, let me neighbour leave me in peace.'

She fumbled in her purse for a fifty pence coin. Should she have the fire on now, in the afternoon, or tonight, while she watched television? It was a decision she made every day except in summer. Troy, her second son, had said, 'Listen, keep the fire on *all* day whenever you need it, Mummy, you only gotta ax for money an' it's yours.'

But Philomena was proud. She dressed slowly in many layers. Then went to the wardrobe where her winter coat hung. She put it on, wound a scarf round her neck, put a felt hat on her head, then, fortified against the cold, went into the kitchen to make her breakfast. She counted the slices of bread: five, and the remaining eggs: three. A bit of marge', but only enough to anoint a baby's head. She shook the box of cornflakes. Half a bowl an' two days to go to pension day. She bent down and opened the door of the refrigerator. 'Waste a time runnin' the t'ing when the air is frozen,' she said. She pulled out the plug and the fridge became silent. She took out a lump of cheese and, with great difficulty (because her hands were knotted and painful with arthritis), she grated cheese onto a slice of bread and put it under the grill.

She waited impatiently, resenting the gas being used. Eventually she removed the cheese on toast before it was properly melted and sat down, in her hat, coat, scarf and gloves, to eat her half-cooked breakfast. Through the wall, she could hear the Queen Mother laughing and furniture being scraped across the floor. She addressed the Queen Mother through the wall: 'You jus' wait, woman. You won't be laughin' soon.'

Philomena had seen Jack Barker on television the night before, explaining that the ex-Royal Family would live on state benefits. That the pensioners, the Queen, Prince Philip and the Queen Mother, would receive the same as Philomena. She closed her eyes and said, 'For what I am about to receive may the Lord make me truly grateful. Amen.' Then she began to eat. She chewed each mouthful carefully, making it last. She would have liked a second slice, but she was saving up for a television licence.

The Queen Mother was laughing at the ridiculous smallness of it all. 'It's a perfectly *adorable* bungalow,' she laughed. 'It's darling. It could be a kennel for a large *dog*.'

She clutched her mink coat to her and inspected

the bathroom. This brought a fresh peal of laughter: displaying teeth that feared the dentist's chair.

'I love it,' she pealed. 'It's so *containable*, and look, Lilibet, there's a hook for one's peignoir.'

The Queen looked at the stainless steel hook on the back of the bathroom door. It was nothing to get excited about; it was simply a hook, a utilitarian object, designed for a purpose; that of hanging one's clothes from.

'There's no lavatory paper, Lilibet,' whispered the Queen Mother. 'How does one obtain lavatory paper?'

She cocked her head to one side coquettishly and waited for an answer.

'One has to buy it from a shop,' said Charles, who was single-handedly emptying the contents of the box van that had recently arrived outside his grandmother's bungalow. He was carrying a standard lamp under one arm and a silk shade under the other.

'*One* does?' The Queen Mother's smile seemed fixed, as though it had been commemorated on Mount Rushmore.

'How simply thrilling.'

'Do you think so?'

The Queen was irritated by her mother's refusal to *give in* to one moment of despair. The bungalow was truly appalling, cramped, smelly and cold. How would her mother *manage*? She had never so much as drawn her own *curtains*. Yet here she was putting a stupidly brave face on this truly awful situation.

Spiggy arrived on his familiar errand and was met with

cries of extravagant greeting. Jack Barker's specifications had been disbelieved by the Queen Mother. A room couldn't be nine feet by nine feet. A digit had been missed out; Barker had meant to write nineteen feet. So large rugs had been removed from Clarence House and transported to Hell Close in the box van. The servants had seen to it – their final act of service: those sober enough to stand.

Spiggy removed the instruments of destruction from his tool bag. Stanley knife, steel measure, black binding tape, and proceeded to cut a precious rug, a present from Persia, to fit around the Queen Mother's orange-tiled fireplace. He was once again the hero of the hour. The Queen Mother promenaded in her back garden, her corgi, Susan, at her side. The black woman next door watched her from her kitchen window. The Queen Mother waved, but the black woman ducked away, out of sight. The Queen Mother's smile faltered slightly, then recovered, like the *Financial Times* Index on a rocky day in the City.

The Queen Mother needed people to love her. People loving her was plasma; without it, she would die. She had lived without a man's love for the greater part of her life. Being adored by the populace was only a small compensation. She was slightly disturbed by her next-door neighbour's unfriendly attitude but, as she came in from the garden her smile was firmly back in place.

She saw Spiggy look up from his labours. There was adoration in his eyes. She engaged him in conversation, enquiring about his wife. 'Run off,' said Spiggy.

'Children?'

'She took 'em wiv 'er.'

'So, you're a gay bachelor?' tinkled the Queen Mother.

Spiggy's brow darkened. 'Who's been sayin' I'm gay?'

Turning to Spiggy, Charles said, 'What Granny meant to say was that you probably have a carefree existence, unshackled by domestic responsibilities.'

'I work hard for my living,' said Spiggy, defensively. 'You wanna try luggin' carpets round all day.'

Charles was discomfited by this misunderstanding. Why couldn't his family simply *talk* to their neighbours without . . . er . . . constant . . . er . . . ?

The Queen handed round delicate china cups and saucers. 'Coffee,' she announced.

Spiggy watched closely to see how the ex-Royals handled the tiny cups. They inserted their forefingers inside the little handles, lifted the saucers and drank. But Spiggy could not get his forefinger, calloused and swollen by years of manual work, to fit inside the handle of his cup. He looked at their hands and compared them to his own. Shamed for a moment, he hid his hands in the pockets of his overalls. He felt himself to be a lumbering beast. Whereas they had a shine on their bodies, sort of like they were covered in glass. Protected, like. Spiggy's body was an illustrated map: accidents at work, fights, neglect, poverty, all had left visible reminders that Spiggy had lived. He grabbed the cup with his right hand and drank the meagre contents. Not enough in one of these to wash a gnat's hat, he grumbled to himself, replacing the little cup on the saucer.

Prince Charles pushed his way out through the small crowd that had gathered outside the Queen Mother's front gate. A youth with a shaved head stood hunched and shivering in the icy wind. He approached Charles.

'You need a video, don't you?'

Charles said, 'Actually, we do rather, that is, my wife does. We left ours behind, didn't think in the, er ... but ... aren't they awfully, er ... well ... expensive?'

'*Normal*, yeah, they are, but I can get 'em for fifty quid.'

'Fifty quid?'

'Yeah, I know this bloke, see, what gets 'em.'

'A philanthropist, is he?'

Warren Deacon stared uncomprehendingly at Charles. 'He's just a bloke.'

'And they, er ... that is ... these video machines, do they ... er ... *work*?'

''Course. They're from good 'omes,' Warren said, indignantly.

Something was puzzling Charles. How did this rodent-faced youth know that they had no video? He asked Warren.

'I walked by your 'ouse las' night. Looked in the winder. No red light. You should draw the curtains. You got some good stuff in there; them candlesticks are the business.'

Charles thanked Warren for the compliment. The youth obviously had a strong aesthetic sense. It really didn't do to judge people too quickly. Charles said, 'They're exquisite, aren't they? William III. He er ... that is, William started his collection in. . . .'

'Solid silver?' enquired Warren.

'Oh yes,' assured Charles. 'Made by Andrew Moore.'

'Oh yeah?' said Warren, as though he was conversant with most of the silversmiths of the seventeenth century.

''Spect they'd fetch a bit then, eh?'

'Probably,' Charles conceded. 'But, as you er . . . may know, we . . . that is . . . my family . . . we aren't allowed to er . . . actually . . . sell any of our er. . . .'

'Stuff?' Warren was getting sick of waiting for Charles to finish his sentences. What a dork! And this bloke was lined up to be King and rule over Warren?

'Yes, stuff.'

'So really, you shoulda lef' the candlesticks be'ind and bought the video?'

'*Brought* the video, yes,' said Charles, pedantically.

'So, you want one?' Warren felt it was time to close the deal.

Charles felt in the pockets of his trousers. He had a fifty pound note somewhere. He found it and handed it over to Warren Deacon. He knew neither Warren's name nor where he lived, but he thought, a boy who is interested in historical artefacts is worth cultivating. He had a vision of showing Warren his small art collection and perhaps encouraging the youth to take up painting. . . .

Charles climbed into the back of the box van and picked up a carton marked 'shoes', but shoes didn't chink and neither did they take a huge effort to lift. Charles opened the lid of the carton and saw twenty-four bottles of Gordon's gin nestling amongst sheets of green tissue paper. He struggled through the small crowd, holding the carton to his chest, sweating with the effort. He wished that Beverley could see him now, carrying such a weight – doing a man's work. When he got to the front door without dropping his heavy burden, the small crowd of women and pushchaired toddlers cheered ironically and Charles, flushed and proud, nodded to acknowledge the cheers, something he had been taught to do since he was three years old.

He staggered into the kitchen with his burden and found his mother washing up at the sink. She was using one hand. Princess Margaret was leaning against the tiny formica table, watching the Queen. Her own household was in chaos. She had nothing suitable to wear. The trunk containing her daytime casual wear had been left in London. Her entire Hell Close wardrobe consisted of six cocktail suits, suitable for show business award ceremonies, but nothing else. She had her furs with her, of course, but this morning a girl with a spider tattooed on her neck had hissed, 'Cowin' animal killer' as they had passed on the pavement outside her new home.

The Queen wanted her out of her mother's kitchen. She was blocking the light and taking up valuable space. There was work to be done.

Spiggy put his head round the door and spoke to Princess Margaret. 'Need any carpets fittin'? I can squeeze you in 's afternoon.'

'Thanks awfully, but no,' she drawled. 'It's hardly worth it, I won't be stopping.'

'Please yourself, Maggie,' said Spiggy, trying to be friendly.

'Maggie?' She pulled herself up to her full height. 'How *dare* you speak to me in that tone. I am Princess Margaret to you.' He thought she was going to hit him. She pulled back a beautifully tailored Karl Lagerfeld sleeve and showed him her fist, but she withdrew it and contented herself with shouting, 'You horrid little fat man,' as she ran back to her Hell Close home.

The Queen put the kettle on. She thought that Mr Spiggy deserved a nice cup of tea. 'I'm so sorry. We're all rather overwrought.'

''S all right,' said Spiggy. 'I *do* need to lose a bit of weight.' Thas' another thing, he thought. None of 'em are fat. Whereas all his relations were fat. The women got fat after they had their kids and the men got fat 'cause of the beer. At Christmas his family could hardly squeeze into their living room. The Queen hummed a tune as they waited for the kettle to boil and Spiggy caught the melody and whistled as he worked on the hall carpet.

'Wa's it called?' he asked the Queen as they came to the end of their impromptu duet.

'*Born Free*,' she replied. 'I saw the film in 1966. A Royal British Film Performance.'

'Free tickets, eh?'

'Yes,' she admitted, 'and no queuing at the box office.'

'Funny though, going to the pictures with a crown on yer 'ead.'

The Queen laughed. 'A tiara! One wouldn't wear a crown; it wouldn't be fair on the person sitting behind.'

Spiggy laughed his booming laugh and Philomena Toussaint banged on the wall and shouted, 'Stop the noise, me head is full of it.'

Philomena was hungry and cold and her head hurt. She was jealous. Her kitchen had been full of laughter once, when the children were at home: Fitzroy, Troy and her baby Jethroe. The food those boys ate! She really needed a bulldozer to fill their mouths: always coming to and from the market she was. She could remember the weight of the basket and the smell of the flat iron as she pressed their damp white shirts for school every morning.

She dragged a chair towards the high cupboard where she kept her packets and tins. She climbed onto the chair and put the cornflakes packet on the top of the cupboard. While she was there, at eye level, she touched and rearranged her tins and packets. Bringing this soup forward, that cereal back, until, satisfied with the adjustments, she lowered herself down from the chair.

'Never had the police at me door,' she said aloud to the empty kitchen. 'And I always got tins in me cupboard,' she said to the hall. 'And there's a place for me in heaven,' she said to the bedroom as she took her coat off and got into bed to keep warm.

By late afternoon, quite a crowd had gathered round the box van, hoping to see the Queen Mother. Inspector Holyland sent a young policeman to move them on. PC Isiah Ludlow would rather have been sent to guard a decomposing corpse than have to face these hard-faced Hell Close women and their malevolent-looking toddlers.

'C'mon now, ladies. Move along, please.' He clapped his big leather police gloves together and that, together with his wispy moustache, gave him the appearance of an eager seal about to be thrown a ball. He repeated his order. None of the women moved.

'You're blocking the thoroughfare.'

None of the women knew for sure what a thoroughfare was. Was it the same as a pavement? A woman, whose pregnant belly strained against her anorak, said, 'We're guardin' the van for the Queen Mother.'

'Well, you can go home now, can't you? I'm here, I'll guard the van.'

The pregnant woman laughed scornfully. 'I wun't trust the police to guard a lump of shit.'

PC Ludlow bridled at this slur on his professional integrity, but he remembered what he had been taught at Hendon. Stay calm, don't let the public get the upper hand. Stay in control.

'It's cos a you my 'usband's doin' two year in Pentonville,' the woman went on.

PC Ludlow should have ignored her remarks but, being young and inexperienced, he said, 'So, he's innocent of any crime, is he?' He'd tried to get a sceptical tone in his voice, but it hadn't quite worked.

The pregnant woman took it as a genuine question. PC Ludlow saw with horror that tears were now dripping down her round, flushed cheeks. Was this what his instructors had called a dialogue with the public?

'They said 'e'd stripped the church roof of all its

lead, but it were a bleedin' lie.' The other women gathered around, patting and stroking the sobbing woman. "'E were frit of heights. It were me 'oo 'ad to stand on a chair to change the light bulbs.'

As Charles emerged from the bungalow, eager to empty the van of its final contents, he heard a woman's voice crying plaintively, 'Les! Les! I want my Les!'

He saw a small group of women surrounding a young policeman. The policeman's helmet fell to the ground and was picked up by a toddler wearing an earring, who put it on his own small head and ran away down the Close.

PC Ludlow tried to explain to the hysterical woman that, though he knew about stitch-ups in the locker room, he had never been a party to one himself. 'Now look here,' he said. He touched the sleeve of her anorak.

The small group moved as one, blocking Charles's entrance to the back of the van. What he now saw was a policeman gripping the arm of a hugely-pregnant young woman who was struggling to be free. He had read accounts of police brutality. Could they possibly be true?

PC Ludlow was now in the centre of the little mob of shouting, shrieking women. If he wasn't careful, he would be knocked off his feet. He hung onto the sleeve of the pregnant woman, whom he now believed to be called Marilyn, according to the shouts of the other members of the mob. Even as he was swayed this way and that, he rehearsed what he would write in his report, because this had now become an 'incident'. Reams of paper stretched ahead of him.

Charles stood on the edge of the group. Should he intervene? He had a reputation for his conciliatory skills. He was convinced that, given the chance, he could have ended the miners' strike. He had wanted to join the University Labour Club at Cambridge, but had been advised against it by Rab Butler. Charles saw Beverley Threadgold slam her front door and race across the road. Her white lycra top, red miniskirt and bare, blue legs gave her the look of a voluptuous union flag.

She ploughed into the group, shouting, 'Leave our Marilyn alone, you cowin' pig.'

PC Ludlow now saw himself in court giving evidence, because Beverley was grappling with him, had him down on the ground. His face was pressed into the pavement, which stank of dogs and cats and nicotine. She was sitting on his back. He could hardly breathe; she was a big woman. With a mighty effort he threw her off. He heard her head hit the ground, then her cry of pain.

'Then, your honour,' said the running commentary in his brain, 'I was aware of a further weight on my back, a man whom I now know to be the former Prince of Wales. This man seemed to be making a frenzied attack on my regulation police overcoat. When asked to stop, he said words to the effect of – "I stood by during the miners' strike, this is for Orgreve." At that point, your honour, Inspector Holyland arrived with reinforcements and several people were arrested, including the former Prince of Wales.

The riot was eventually stopped at eighteen hundred hours.'

During the riot, the remaining contents of the box van were stolen by Warren Deacon and his small brother, Hussein. The Gainsboroughs, Constables and assorted sporting oils were sold to the landlord of the local pub, the Yuri Gagarin, for a pound each. Mine host was refurbishing the smoke room, turning it Olde Worlde. The paintings would look all right next to the warming pans and horns of plenty stuffed with dried flowers.

Later, the Queen tried to comfort her mother on her loss by saying, 'I've got a nice Rembrandt; you can have that. It would look nice over the fireplace; shall I fetch it, Mummy?'

'No, don't leave me, Lilibet. I can't be left; I've never been alone.' The Queen Mother clutched her elder daughter's hand.

Night had long since fallen. The Queen was tired, she craved the oblivion of sleep. It had taken forever to undress her mother and prepare her for bed and there was still so much to *do*. Ring the police station, comfort Diana, prepare a meal for Philip and herself. She longed to see Anne. Anne was a bulwark.

She could hear inane studio audience laughter through the wall. Perhaps the next-door neighbour would stay with her mother until she went to sleep? She gently withdrew her mother's hand and, under the guise of giving Susan a bowl of Go-dog in the kitchen, she quietly let herself out of the bungalow and went next door and rang the bell.

Philomena answered the door wearing her coat, hat, scarf and gloves.

'Oh,' said the Queen. 'Are you going out?'

'No, I just come in,' lied Philomena, shocked to see the Queen of England and the Commonwealth at the door. The Queen explained her dilemma, stressing her mother's great age.

'I'll help you outta' your trouble, woman. I see your son bein' took by the police, bringin' shame on his family.'

The Queen, humbled, muttered her thanks and went to break the news to her mother that she would not be spending the night alone; Mrs Philomena Toussaint, former hospital cleaner, teetotaller and Episcopalian, would be sitting by the gas fire in the living room next door; but there were four conditions. While she was in the house, there was to be no drinking, gambling, drug taking or blasphemy. The Queen Mother agreed to these conditions and the two old women were introduced.

'We met before, in Jamaica,' said Philomena. 'I was wearing a red dress and wavin' a little flag.'

The Queen Mother played for time. 'Ah now, what year would that be?' she said.

Philomena rummaged about in her memory. The ticking of the Sèvres clock on the dressing table served to accentuate the distance and the time that the two old women were trying to bridge.

'1927?' said the Queen Mother, vaguely remembering a West Indian Tour.

'So you remember me?' Philomena was pleased. 'Your husband, what's 's name?'

'George.'

'Yes, that's the one, George. I was sorry when he was took by God.'

'Yes, so was I,' admitted the Queen Mother. 'I was rather cross with God at the time.'

'When God took my husband away, I stopped goin' to church,' admitted Philomena. 'The man beat me and took me money for drink, but I missed him. Did George beat you?' The Queen Mother said no, that George had never beaten her, that, having been beaten himself as a child, he hated violence. He was a dear, sweet man and he hadn't particularly enjoyed being King.

'See,' said Philomena, 'that's why the Lord took him; to give the man some peace.'

The Queen Mother settled back onto the fine linen pillowcases and closed her eyes, and Philomena took off her outdoor clothing and sat by the fire on a fine gilt armchair, relishing the free heat.

Charles was allowed to make one phone call. Diana was emulsioning the kitchen walls when the phone rang. A constipated voice said, 'Mrs Teck? Tulip Road Police Station here. Your husband is on the line.' She heard Charles's voice, 'Listen, I'm awfully sorry about all this.'

Diana said, 'Charles, I couldn't *believe* it when Wilf Toby came round and said you'd been fighting in the street. I was painting the bathroom. Aqua Green looks *stupendous*, by the way – I'm going to try and get a matching shower curtain. Anyway, I had my Sony on and missed all the excitement. You being arrested, thrown in the black maria; but I let the boys stay up and watch the rest of the riot. Oh, that boy Warren came round with the video. I paid him fifty quid.'

Charles said, 'But *I* paid him fifty quid.'

Diana carried on as though he hadn't spoken, he had never heard her so animated.

'It works beautifully. I'm going to watch *Casablanca* before I go to bed.'

Charles said, 'Listen, darling, it's frightfully important, could you phone our solicitor for me? I'm about to be charged with affray.'

Diana heard a voice say, 'That's enough, Teck, back to your cell.'

11 Knob

Charles was sharing a cell with a tall thin youth called Lee Christmas. When Charles entered the cell, Lee turned his lugubrious face, stared at Charles and said, 'You Prince Charles?'

Charles said, 'No, I'm Charlie Teck.'

Lee said, 'Watcha in for?'

Charles said, 'Affray and assaulting a police officer.'

'Yeah? Bit posh for that, ain't yer?'

Charles diverted this uncomfortable line of questioning and asked, 'You are er . . . in for?'

'I stole a knob.'

'Stole a knob?' Charles pondered on this. Was it a piece of arcane criminal jargon? Had Mr Christmas committed some unsavoury type of sexual offence? If so, it was disgraceful that he, Charlie, was being forced to share a cell with him. Charles pressed against the cell door. He kept his eye on the buzzer.

'There was this car, right? Bin in our street over free months; tyres an' stereo went first night. Then everythin' went, 'cludin' engine. 'S a shell, right?'

Charles nodded, he could see the wreck in his mind's eye. There was one just like it in Hell Close. William and Harry played in it. 'Any road up,' continued Lee. 'It's a Renault, right? An' I got one the same. More or less the same year – so, I'm walkin' by,

right? An' there's kids playin' in this wreck 'tendin'
to be Cinderella on their way to the – wassa place?'

'Ball?' offered Charles.

'Dance, disco,' corrected Lee. 'Any road, I tell 'em
to fuck off an' I get in the front – seats are gone – an'
I'm jus' pullin' this knob off the top of the gear lever,
right? 'Cos the knob's missin' off mine, see? So I want
it, OK?' Charles grasped the point Lee was making.

'When 'oo d' ya think grabs me arm through the
winder?' Lee waited. Charles stammered, 'Without
knowing your circumstances, Mr Christmas, your
family, friends or acquaintances, it's frightfully difficult
to guess who may have. . . .'

'The *bogus beasts*,' shouted Lee indignantly. 'Two
coppers in plain clothes,' he explained, looking at
Charles's baffled expression. 'An' I'm arrested for
thieving from this piece of *shrapnel*. A knob, a bleedin'
knob. Worth thirty-seven cowin' pee.'

Charles was appalled, 'But that's simply appalling,'
he said.

'Worse thing 's ever 'appened to me,' said Lee.
''Cludin the dog gettin' run over. I'm a joke in our
family. When I get out of 'ere I'll 'ave ter do summat
big. Post Office or summat like that. ''Less I do, I'll
never be able to 'old me 'ead up in the Close again.'

'Where do you live?' asked Charles.

'Hell Close,' said Lee Christmas. 'Your sister's
gonna be our nex' door neighbour. We 'ad a letter
tellin' us not to curtsey 'n' stuff.'

'No, no, you mustn't,' insisted Charles. 'We're ordinary citizens now.'

'All the same, our mam's 'avin' a perm at the

hairdressers, an' she's goin' mad, cleanin' an' stuff. She's a lazy cow, normal. She's like your mum – never does no 'ousework.'

There was a jangle of keys and the cell door opened and a policeman came in with a tray. He handed Lee a plate of sandwiches covered in clingfilm, saying, ''Ere Christmas, get that down your neck.'

To Charles he said, 'Tricky stuff that clingfilm, sir, allow me to remove it.'

Before he left the cell he had addressed Charles as 'sir' six times and had also wished him 'a good night's sleep' and had slipped him a mini pack of Jaffa cakes.

Lee Christmas said, ''S true then?'

'What's true?' asked Charles, his mouth full of bread, cheese and pickle.

''S one law for the cowin' rich and one for the cowin' poor.'

'Sorry,' said Charles, and he gave Lee a Jaffa cake.

At eleven o'clock, Radio Two burst into the cell and filled the small space. Charles and Lee covered their ears against the earsplitting volume. Charles pressed the buzzer repeatedly, but nobody came, not even the deferential policeman for the tray.

Lee bellowed, 'Turn it down!' through the slot in the door. They could hear other prisoners shouting for mercy. 'This is torture,' shouted Charles over 'Shrimp Boats Are A Comin'. But there was worse to come. Some unseen person adjusted the tuning knob and the radio blared out, 'He's Got The Whole World In His Hands' even louder, complete with piercing static, and in the background what sounded like a Serbo-Croatian phone-in.

Charles had often wondered how he would stand up to torture. Now he knew. Given five minutes of such audio hell, he would crack and turn his own sons over to the authorities. He tried mind over matter and went through the Kings and Queens of England since the year 802: Egbert, Ethelwulf, Ethelbald, Ethelbert, Ethelred, Alfred the Great, Edward the Elder, Athelstan, Edmund I, Edred, Edwy, Edgar, Edward II the Martyr – but he gave up on the Saxons and Danes, unable to remember whether Harold Harefoot ruled alone or jointly with Hardicanute in 1037. When he reached the House of Plantagenet – Edward I, Longshanks – he drifted off to sleep wondering how tall *exactly* Longshanks was. But Shirley Bassey woke him with 'Diamonds Are Forever', and he continued his list: House of Saxe-Coburg and Gotha: Edward VII, then sped through the House of Windsor – George V; Edward VIII; George VI; Elizabeth II – until he came to an empty space. At some time in the future, after his mother's death, it would have been him: captive in quite a different prison.

Meanwhile Lee Christmas slept, clutching his shoulders with his thin hands, his knees drawn up to his concave belly, his humiliation forgotten. His Renault car on the road, pristine, gleaming, a girl at his side, his hand on the fatal knob, about to change gear.

The Queen lay awake, worrying about her son. She had once inadvertently watched a BBC2 Bristol documentary about hooliganism (she had expected it to be about wild animals). A famous vet had drawn a connection between maternal deprivation and violence. Was that why Charles had started fighting in the street? Was it her fault? She hadn't wanted to go on those world tours and leave Charles behind, but in those days she had believed her advisers when they assured her that the British export trade would collapse without her support. Well, it had collapsed anyway, she thought bitterly. She might just as well have stayed at home with the dogs and seen Charles for a couple of hours a day.

Another problem was keeping the Queen awake: she was running out of money. Somebody from the Department of Social Security was supposed to call and bring her some more, but hadn't turned up. How was she supposed to get to the Magistrates' Court in the morning without a car or taxi fare?

After searching Philip's trouser pockets and finding nothing, she had called on her relatives and asked for a loan of ten pounds. But the Queen Mother couldn't find her purse. Princess Margaret pretended not to be in, though the Queen distinctly saw her shadow behind the frosted glass of the front door, and Diana had spent her initial emergency payment on paint and a video machine apparently.

The Queen couldn't understand where her own money had all gone. How did one *manage*? She turned the bedside light on and, using paper and a pencil, tried to tot up her expenses since moving into Hell Close. She got as far as: 'Mr Spiggy – £50' before the light went out. The electricity meter needed feeding, but having nothing to feed it with, the Queen settled for darkness.

Crawfie spoke to her. 'C'mon now, Lilibet, hat

and coat and gloves on, we're going to ride on the Underground.' She and Margaret and Crawfie had once travelled from Piccadilly Circus to Tottenham Court Road, changing at Leicester Square. Thrillingly, the lights in the carriage had gone out several times during the journey. She had reported this to her parents as being the most exciting part of the excursion, but her parents had not shared her pleasure. To them, darkness represented danger and Crawfie was forbidden to repeat the experiment of taking the young princesses into the real world of imperfect people, who wore drab clothes and spoke another language.

12 Porky Pies

The Queen looked at her son in the dock and remembered the last time she had seen him behind bars. He'd been in his playpen in the nursery wing at Buckingham Palace. Diana sat next to her, clutching a wet handkerchief. Her eyes and nose were pink. Why had she forgotten to ask a solicitor to go and see Charles at the police station? How could such an important thing have slipped her mind? It was entirely her fault that Charles was now being represented by the court Duty Solicitor, Oliver Meredith Lebutt, a red-haired, disreputable-looking man with nicotined fingers and a speech impediment. The Queen had taken an instant dislike to him. Charles waved and smiled at his wife and mother in the public gallery and was rebuked by the Chief Magistrate, a stern Trade Unionist called Tony Wrigglesworth.

'This is not a carnival, Mr Teck.'

The Queen pricked her ears. 'Teck?' Why was Charles using his great-grandmother's maiden name? Thank God Philip had refused to get out of bed and come to the Magistrates' Court. It could, quite possibly, have killed him.

Diana smiled back at her husband, he looked *great*. Two days' stubble gave him the fabulous *raunchy* look of the street fightin' man. She winked at her husband and he winked back, provoking another rebuke from Tony Wrigglesworth. 'Mr Teck, you are not the comedian Rowan Atkinson, so please refrain from indulging in facial contortions.'

Sycophantic laughter rippled around the court. However, it did not ripple along the press bench, because the press were absent. The streets around the court were closed to traffic and pedestrians and, in particular, media personnel.

There was a sudden commotion and Beverley Threadgold came up the stairs from the cells below and joined Charles in the dock. Beverley was hand-cuffed to a policewoman. Charles, who was still standing, turned to Beverley and offered her a chair. Tony Wrigglesworth thumped the bench in rage and shouted, 'Teck, you are not a furniture salesman! Remain standing, Mrs Threadgold.'

Charles helped Beverley to her feet. Seeing their hands touch gave Diana a pang of jealousy. Beverley did look fabulous in the dock, curvy and womanly in a knitted two-piece. Diana resolved to put on at least a stone in weight.

The third prisoner was brought up – Violet Toby, looking pale and old without her make-up. Tony Threadgold and Wilf Toby nodded their heads towards their wives, too afraid of Tony Wrigglesworth for anything more friendly.

The case began. The Crown Prosecutor, a dumpy head-girl type of woman called Susan Bell, gave the facts to the court. The Queen, who had been a witness to the events described in such dramatic terms by Ms Bell, was horrified. It simply wasn't *true*. PC Ludlow was called and told lies, claiming he was savagely assaulted by Charles, Beverley and Violet.

No, he couldn't explain the reason for this assault. Perhaps it was the influence of television. Inspector Holyland backed PC Ludlow's story, calling the so-called attack on Ludlow 'an orgy of violence, led by the man, Teck, who had been heard to shout, "Kill the pig".'

Tony Wrigglesworth intervened, 'And there was not a pig in the immediate vicinity, a four-legged pig?'

'No sir, I believed Teck's phrase, "Kill the pig", to mean that he was urging his accomplices to murder PC Ludlow.'

The Queen said very loudly, 'Nonsense.' Wrigglesworth was on to her immediately.

'Madam, this is not a fringe theatre. We do not encourage audience participation.'

Oliver Meredith Lebutt stopped exploring the wax in his ears and put a waxy finger to his lips, indicating to the Queen that she must remain silent. The Queen was overwhelmed with feelings of rage and hatred, but she kept her silence and merely scowled at the bench where Tony Wrigglesworth was conferring with his fellow magistrates, one a tweedy box of a woman, the other a nervous man in an ill-fitting Next suit.

The hearing continued, the sun came out and the trio in the dock were illuminated from behind, which gave them the look of angels descending from heaven.

Oliver Meredith Lebutt lumbered to his feet, dropped his papers and, in his high, lisping voice, proceeded to address his clients by the wrong names, mix up their evidence and generally antagonise the court. It was a surprise to everyone when, after a short adjournment, Tony Wrigglesworth announced that all three defendants would go to trial at the Crown Court, but would be granted bail, providing certain conditions could be met.

Oliver Meredith Lebutt punched the air in triumph as though he had won a major victory at the Old Bailey. He looked around expecting congratulations, but when nobody came forward he shuffled his papers together and lurched out of the courtroom to flirt with Susan Bell, the Crown Prosecutor, with whom he was falling in love.

Charles insisted on staying in court to hear the next case. Lee Christmas was sent to prison for two months for the theft of a black plastic knob. Before he went down to begin his sentence he shouted, 'Tell our mam not to worry, Charlie,' which prompted Tony Wrigglesworth to declare that the court was not a message service.

As they left the Court and walked along the abnormally quiet street outside, Tony Threadgold suggested that they should have a celebratory cup of tea at the British Home Stores before catching the bus back to Hell Close. The Queen felt quite lonely as she watched the three couples enter the café in front of her. Wilf had his hand on Violet's shoulder. Tony and Beverley were hand in hand and Diana had snuggled her head into Charles's shoulder. All the Queen had for comfort was her black patent handbag.

She had expected that the public appearance of three members of the ex-Royal Family would cause a sensation in the crowded café but, apart from a few curious glances at Charles's dishevelled appearance and Diana's Ray Bans worn in April, nobody took particular notice. There were many women of the Queen's age seated at the formica tables, most of them headscarfed and wearing brooches pinned to their coats. The Queen said: 'I'm afraid I have no money to pay for the tea.'

Tony said, 'No sweat,' and, after urging the rest of the group to find a table, went to queue at the self-service counter. He came back with seven cups of tea and seven doughnuts. Beverley said, 'Tone, you're lovely, you really are.'

The Queen agreed. She was ravenous. She bit hungrily into the doughnut and jam dripped out and trickled down the front of her cashmere coat.

Violet handed her a paper napkin and said, "Ere, 'ave a serviette, Liz.' And the Queen, instead of taking offence at the over-familiarity, thanked Violet, took the napkin and wiped her coat.

13 Grid Marks

When Charles got back to Hell Close he went to see Mrs Christmas to relay the message from her son. He found the house in uproar. Mr and Mrs Christmas were in the middle of a violent row with the six teenage sons – something about missing rent money. Mrs Christmas had one son in a judo hold, round his neck. Mr Christmas was brandishing a potato masher towards the others. The son who had let Charles into the house leapt back into the argument, as though he had never left, proclaiming his innocence at full volume. 'Well, it weren't me!'

'Well, all I know is I left that rent money under the clock an' now it's gone,' said Mrs Christmas.

Mr Christmas jabbed the potato masher towards his sons and said, 'An' one of *you* bastards 'as 'ad it.'

The sons became quiet. Two of them already had grid marks on their foreheads. Even Charles's heart beat loudly in his breast and he *certainly* hadn't had the rent money.

Mr Christmas began to prowl around the living room and spoke, as though he were giving a lecture to particularly dim university students. 'Now I know I ain't an angel. Fact is, I'm a tea leaf, no sense in 'idin' it. And 'til recent I've kep' you all in food and clothes and shoes, ain't I?'

'They've gone without nothink,' said Mrs Christmas loyally. 'They've 'ad everythink they've ever wanted, father.' She released her hold on her son's neck and he fell away from her, retching.

Mr Christmas continued his address. 'OK, so I've broke the law of the land, but I ain't never broke a more important law, which is you never shit on your own patch. You don't thieve off your neighbours and you *never* thieve off your own family.' Mr Christmas looked around at his sons, profoundly moved by his own oratory, his eyes misted over. 'I know things 've been 'ard since I done me back in.'

Mrs Christmas defended her husband fiercely, 'How's he supposed to break an' enter with 'is back in a corset?'

Charles began to feel sorry for Mr Christmas, a fellow back sufferer deprived of his livelihood. He cleared his throat. The Christmas family turned towards him, expecting him to speak. Charles stammered, 'So, Mr Christmas, what do you blame for this deterioration of the morality of the criminal classes?'

Mr Christmas hadn't understood the question so he waved the potato masher vaguely towards the living room window and the street beyond.

Charles said excitedly, 'Society! Yes, I totally agree with you. The breakdown of educational standards and er . . . the disparity between rich and poor. . . .'

A large pantechnicon drove slowly by the Christmas's window, blocking the light. It parked next door. Charles looked out and saw that his sister was at the wheel. Mrs Christmas rushed to the mantelpiece and began to titivate her tight blue curls. She threw her apron into a corner and changed out of her slippers and into white wedge-heeled sandals. She turned to her six sons and her husband and said, 'So, *what* do you say when you meet 'er?'

Seven sonorous voices said as one: ''Ello your Royal 'Ighness. Welcome to 'Ell Close.'

'Yes,' breathed Mrs Christmas. 'I'm proud on yer.'

Charles said, 'Oh Mrs Christmas, I've bad news, I'm afraid. Lee got sent down for two months.'

Mrs Christmas sighed and said to her husband, 'You'll have to eat his chop, then. Can you manage three?'

Mr Christmas assured his wife that Lee's chop wouldn't be wasted. Then they all trooped outside and stood at their paint-blistered gate to watch Charles welcome his sister to Hell Close.

'Wotcha,' said Anne. 'This is a bloody hole. You look awful. Who're the dorks at the gate?'

'Your neighbours.'

'Christ! They look like the Munsters.'

'They're not monsters, Anne, they're. . . .'

'*Munsters* – you know, on the telly. . . .'

'I don't watch. . . .'

'How's Mum?'

Anne let down the ramp at the back of the van and her children, Peter and Zara, staggered out looking pale and ill. Anne said, 'I bloody well told you you wouldn't enjoy it in the back, but you wouldn't listen, would you?' She threw the keys to Seven Hell Close to Peter and told him to open the front door. She ordered Zara to take the dog for a walk and instructed Charles to start emptying the van. She strode around to the front of the van, woke the driver, who was sitting in the passenger seat and then went to introduce herself to the Christmas family.

To her astonishment, the Munster woman and the Munster men said, in Munster voices: "Ello, your Royal 'Ighness, welcome to 'Ell Close.' She shook eight hands and said, 'My name is Anne. Call me that, would ya', please!'

Mrs Christmas practically swooned with delight and dropped into a curtsey, bending her fat knees and bowing her head, but when she arose from abasing herself in front of the Princess, she was disturbed to find that Princess Anne was curtseying to *her*, Winnie Christmas. She didn't know what to make of it. It put her at sixes and sevens. What did it mean? Was she taking the piss? But no. She looked dead serious. *Dead* serious. As though Winnie was as good as *she* was. I mean.

The Queen hurried down the Close when she heard that Anne had arrived. She threw herself into her daughter's arms with uncharacteristic passion. 'I'm so, so pleased to see you,' the Queen said.

Charles stood by. He felt useless and stupid. There was something about Anne that made him feel ... he groped for the word ... foolish? No. Effete? Yes. Nearer the mark. Unlike him, she despised the speculative, preferring practical, down-to-earth solutions to everyday problems. In the past she had openly mocked his attempts to make sense of the world. He felt lonely. Where would he find a fellow spirit in Hell Close?

Anne's home was much like the other houses in Hell Close, but, being on a corner site, had an unusually large garden, which was full of brambles. The house was dirty, damp, cold and cramped, but she declared herself satisfied with it. 'It's a roof over one's head,' she said. 'It's better than being put up against a wall and shot.'

The Christmas sons, Craig, Wayne, Darren, Barry, Mario and Englebert were put to emptying the van. Mrs Christmas sent Mr Christmas to the shop to buy a packet of Flash and a plastic mop bucket. While he was gone on his errand, she and Anne swept the mouse droppings off the floors.

Peter and Zara were taken next door to watch the Christmas's vast television set. As they entered the living room they were unable to stop their noses from wrinkling. The Christmas's vast black cat, Sonny, lay in a cardboard box on an acrylic cardigan. He was old and incontinent but, as Mrs Christmas explained to the children, 'I'm not 'avin' 'im put down; what's a bit of a stink matter?' She approached Sonny and stroked his mangy head. 'You want to die at 'ome, don't you?'

The children cheered up slightly. The Christmas family were awfully common, but at least they liked animals, so they couldn't be all bad. They had watched their mother weeping this morning as she said goodbye to her horses. They had tried to comfort her, but she had pushed them away and dried her eyes and said, 'Always a mistake to get too attached to one's animals.'

Zara held her nose and crouched at the side of Sonny's basket. She rearranged the urine-soaked cardigan while Peter zapped through thirty-six channels of cable television. Sonny blinked his dying eyes as the channels flicked by. He could smell mice, but he hadn't the strength to climb out of his basket and do his duty.

Meanwhile, the mice gambolled inside the cavity in the party wall between the two houses, waiting for Anne's groceries to be unpacked and put away in the pantry.

Spiggy turned up, expecting to carve up Anne's carpets. But his skills were not needed. Unlike the others, Anne had taken Jack Barker's measurements seriously. Her carpets and furniture were modest, both in taste and size. Mrs Christmas, who had expected luxury beyond her wildest dreams, was bitterly disappointed. Where was the gold and silver plate? The velvet curtains? The silk-covered chairs? The high beds with the brocade hangings? And where was all them fantastic evening frocks an' tiaras? Anne's wardrobe was full of trousers an' jeans an' jackets the colour of pond slime. Mrs Christmas felt cheated. 'I mean,' she said later to Mr Christmas, as she peeled ten pounds of potatoes for their dinner, 'What are the Royal Family *for* if they're goin' to be jus' like ordinary people?'

'Dunno,' said Mr Christmas, as he arranged nineteen tiny breast of lamb chops onto a filthy grill pan. 'But they ain't the Royal Family no more, thassa point, 'ent it?'

From next door came the sound of pipes banging, as the former Princess Royal plumbed her washing machine in, using Tony Threadgold's toolbox and the *Reader's Digest D.I.Y. Manual.*

14 The Pack

Harris was running so fast that he thought his heart and lungs would burst. Ahead of him was the Pack: the leader, King, an alsatian; Raver, the deputy leader; Kylie, the Pack bitch; and Lovejoy, Mick and Duffy, ordinary low-status dogs like himself. King stopped and urinated up against the Community Centre wall, and the others sat for a while until Harris joined them. Then, after a brief mock fight, they were off again, heading toward the Recreation Ground. Harris ran alongside Duffy, whose mother was a kerry blue and whose father was unknown. Duffy was a good scrapper, Harris had seen him in action.

King led the Pack across the road, causing a Meals on Wheels van to screech to a halt. Harris followed; he had been taught to sit at the kerb, but he knew that if he did that now he would lose all credibility with the Pack. Tough dogs don't look right or left. From the safety of the pavement he turned and bared his teeth at the white-faced driver of the van, a mild-looking, middle-aged woman. Then Raver barked and they were off again, running in the direction of the children's play area, with its smashed equipment and concrete surface littered with broken glass and sweet wrappings.

Lovejoy, the feeble-minded labrador and Mick, the lurcher, sniffed around Kylie, who ran to King for protection. Mick snapped at Lovejoy's tail and Lovejoy snapped back and soon both dogs were rolling in the grass in a snarling vicious ball. Harris hoped he wouldn't have to take sides. He had no experience of street fighting. He'd been kept on a lead for most of his life. He realised as he watched King and Raver join in the fight that he had, until now, led an extremely sheltered existence. Then, for no reason that Harris could see, the fight stopped and each dog sat down to lick its wounds.

Harris lay on the grass next to Kylie. She was a pretty dog. A honey-coloured cross-collie. True, she could have done with a good grooming; her hair was matted with mud. But Harris was excited by her proximity. He had never been allowed to breed with anybody of *his* choice before. All his previous liaisons had been arranged for him by the Queen. It was time he had some romance in his life, he thought.

He was edging nearer to Kylie when King got to his feet and pricked his ears and stared at the far end of the Recreation Ground, where a strange dog could be seen in the distance. Harris recognised the intruder immediately. It was Susan, his half sister, running slightly ahead of Philomena Toussaint and the Queen Mother, who were strolling arm-in-arm, enjoying the spring sunshine. Harris had never liked Susan. She was a snob and, anyway, he was jealous of her fancy wardrobe. Look at her now, wearing her poncy tartan coat. What *did* she look like? Harris saw an opportunity to enhance his status with the Pack and he left the line and ran towards Susan, barking furiously. Susan turned tail and ran back towards the Queen Mother, but she wasn't a match for Harris, who easily caught up with her and bit her hard on her nose. The Queen Mother swiped at Harris with the walking stick she was carrying and shouted, 'Harris, you horrid little dog!'

As Harris retreated, Philomena threw a small stone that hit him behind his left ear, but he didn't care about the pain. It was worth it to receive the signals of congratulation from the Pack. Harris was promoted and allowed to run behind Raver as they left the Recreation Ground and headed towards the chip shop dustbins which sometimes held delicious fishy scraps.

When Harris returned home late that night, smelling of fish, covered in mud and with dried blood behind his ear, the Queen said, 'You're nothing but a stinking hooligan, Harris!'

Harris thought, hey, I don't have to *take* this. I'm number three in the Pack now, baby. He strolled jauntily into the kitchen expecting to see his food in his bowl, but his bowl was empty. The Queen picked him up and took him upstairs to the bathroom. She locked the door, turned the bath taps on, added the last of her Crabtree and Evelyn's bath lotion, waited until there was sufficient water in the tub and then hurled the protesting Harris into the foaming bubbles.

In the next door bathroom, Beverley Threadgold said to her husband, 'Tone, what's she *doin'* to that poor dog?' Tony said: 'Killin' it, I 'ope.' Harris had been using the Threadgolds' back garden as a lavatory.

'Anyway,' said Beverley, standing up in the bath, naked and lovely. 'It's time you 'ad the taps.'

15 Lonesome Tonight

The following evening, the Queen climbed over the broken fence and rang the Threadgolds' front door bell. A few notes of 'Are You Lonesome Tonight?' chimed through the house. Beverley opened the door wearing burgundy mock velvet pyjamas with white elasticated cuffs at wrist and ankle. She was barefoot and the Queen noticed that Beverley's toenails were a curious atrophied yellow colour. The Queen held out a five pound note: 'I'm repaying the money your husband so kindly lent to me: for bus fares and the gas meter.'

'Come in,' said Beverley, and led the Queen through the hall into the small kitchen. It was the first time the Queen had been in their house. Elvis Presley was everywhere; in pictures, on the wall, on plates, cups and saucers in a cupboard. On tea towels drying from an overhead rack. On an apron hanging from the back of the door. The kitchen curtains bore his face. The mat under the Queen's feet showed him in his notorious pelvic thrust pose.

Tony Threadgold stubbed out his cigarette in Elvis's left eye and got to his feet as the Queen entered. The Queen handed Tony the five pound note, saying, 'I'm most grateful, Mr Threadgold. My mother finally found her purse in the gas oven.' Tony cleared a pile of Elvis boxer shorts from a stool and asked the Queen to sit down. Beverley filled the Presley kettle and the Queen said, 'I see you're fans of Elvis Presley.'

The Threadgolds agreed that they were. When the tea was mashed, they went through to the living room and the Queen was introduced to the most precious pieces of Elvis memorabilia. But the Queen's eye was taken by a lurid oil painting of two young children which hung over the fireplace. The Queen asked who they were. There was a slight pause, then Tony said, 'It's Vernon and Lisa, our kids. We thought it was worth 'aving 'em painted. It'll be an heirloom in years to come.' The Queen was surprised; she had assumed that the Threadgolds were childless. She said so. Beverley said, 'No, we got kids but they've bin took off us.' The Queen asked, 'By whom?'

Tony said, 'Social Services, they've 'ad 'em eighteen month.' He and Beverley drew together and looked at the beautiful painted faces of their children. The Queen did not like to question them further and they did not volunteer any more information so the Queen thanked them for the tea and said goodnight. Tony saw her out and waited until she was safely at her own front door. The Queen said to him across the fence, as she took out her key, 'I'm sure that you and Mrs Threadgold were excellent parents.'

'Thanks,' said Tony, and he closed his door and went to comfort his wife. The Queen went upstairs and opened the bedroom door a few inches and peered inside. Her husband was lying on his side. He opened his eyes and looked at her with such an expression of misery that she went to the bed and took his grimy hand.

'Philip, what is it?'

'I've lost everything,' he said. 'What's the point in living?'

'What is it that you miss particularly, my darling?' The Queen stroked her husband's unshaven cheek. How *old* he looks today, she thought.

'I miss every bloody thing, warmth, softness, comfort, beauty, the cars, the carriages, the servants, the food, the *space*. I can't breathe in this hideous box of a house. I miss my office and the royal train and the plane and the *Britannia*. I don't like the people in Hell Close, Lilibet. They're ugly. They can't talk properly. They smell. I'm frightened of them. I refuse to mix with them. I shall stay in bed until I die.'

The Queen thought, he sounds like a *child*. She said, 'I'm going to heat a tin of soup, would you like some?' Philip whined, 'Not hungry!' and turned his back on his wife. The Queen went downstairs to make her supper. As she stood stirring her Baxter's game soup, she heard the heartbreaking sound of Beverley Threadgold sobbing through the party wall. The Queen bit her lip, but a single sympathetic tear rolled down her face and dripped into the saucepan. The Queen quickly stirred this evidence of her lack of control into the soup. At least I won't need to add salt, she thought. And there were no witnesses. Harris scrabbled at the kitchen door, hungry after a seven mile run with the Pack. The Queen had not been able to afford to buy dog food, so she poured some of the soup into his food bowl and broke a slice of stale bread into pieces to add a little bulk.

Harris looked on with disgust. Just what was happening here? His social life had improved but the food had become a joke. A joke! The Queen said, 'I'll buy you some bones tomorrow, Harris, that's a promise. Now you eat your soup and bread and I'll eat mine.'

Harris looked at her with a malevolence that the Queen had never seen in him before. He growled at the back of his throat, his eyes became slits, he bared his teeth and moved towards the Queen's slim ankles. She kicked out at him before he could bite her. He retreated behind the kitchen door. 'Your behaviour is intolerable, Harris. From now on I forbid you to mix with those frightful mongrels. They are a bad influence on you. You used to be such a nice little dog!'

Harris curled his lip like a sullen teenager. He had never been a nice little dog. The footmen hated him and he had enjoyed tormenting them, tangling his lead, urinating in the corridors and knocking his water bowl over. But these were minor crimes compared with his sneaky habit of taking nips at their vulnerable ankles. Harris had exploited his position as the Queen's favourite. There had been a time when he could do no wrong. Until tonight. He decided it would be politic to hang about the house for a few days, ask the Queen's pardon, be a nice little dog. He came out from behind the door and began to lap politely at his soup.

16 Leslie Makes her Entrance

In the early hours of the following morning Marilyn, common-law wife of the imprisoned Les, gave birth to her first child. Violet Toby acted as midwife. She had been sent for as soon as Marilyn's waters had broken. Marilyn hadn't elected to have a home birth. She was especially looking forward to three days in the Maternity Hospital, but the ambulance, misdirected by the computer, lost its way in the maze of the Flowers Estate. When Violet realised that the baby's arrival was imminent, she looked out of the window in Marilyn's living room to see who was still up in Hell Close. There was a chink of light showing through the Queen's velvet curtains. So Violet reassured Marilyn, who was crying out in pain, that she was going for assistance and ran outside and knocked on the Queen's front door.

The Queen looked through the curtains and saw Violet Toby on her doorstep, wearing a Burgundy candlewick dressing gown and plimsolls. The Queen was doing a jigsaw, she held a piece of Balmoral cloud in her hand. As she went to answer the door, she saw where the piece belonged and slotted it into place.

'I need 'elp,' said Violet, panting from the short run. 'Marilyn's baby's comin' an' there's only a daft teenager in the 'ouse.'

The Queen protested that she had no experience of maternity procedures, she would be 'useless, only get in the way'. But Violet insisted and the Queen reluctantly followed her down the street and into Marilyn's living room. The daft teenager, one of Les's children by a previous liaison, stood over Marilyn with a wet dishcloth, a grey slimy piece of cloth taken unrinsed from the kitchen sink. 'I said *face cloth*, you great gorm,' said Violet and sent him upstairs to the bathroom, shouting after him, 'An' find some clean sheets!'

'There ain't no clean sheets,' he shouted down.

Marilyn contorted herself on the dirt-glazed sofa, which was draped with clothes waiting to be washed. Violet threw the stinking clothes aside, put Marilyn on her back and took her knickers off. The Queen had watched enough cowboy films to know that hot water would be needed and she went to find a kettle and a clean bowl. The kitchen was spectacularly squalid. It was evident that whoever was in charge of keeping the house had failed to do so for rather a long time.

The Queen could not bring herself to touch any of the objects in the room, coated as they all were in grease and dirt. Her feet stuck to the filthy tiled floor. There was no kettle, only a blackened saucepan standing on a fat-encrusted stove.

As she turned to go out, her eye was caught by a bright splash of colour. On a shelf, too high for the squalor to have reached, somebody had placed a three pack of babies' vests – yellow, turquoise and green. The Queen stood on tiptoe and knocked the plastic package down. For some reason, the vests made her throat constrict. 'I'm going home,' she said.

'Don't leave me now, it'll be 'ere any minute,' pleaded Violet. Marilyn was shrieking with each contraction, 'I want Les, I want Les.'

'I'll be back,' promised the Queen. She ran back to her house and collected linen sheets, towels and pillowcases, a silver kettle, cups and saucers, tea and milk, a large fifteenth-century porcelain bowl and baby clothes that had once belonged to her great-grandmother, Queen Victoria. She had brought them with her from Buckingham Palace. She knew that Diana was keen to have a daughter.

Philip stirred as she banged about in the bedroom, searching the cardboard boxes for baby clothes. How squalid he looks, thought the Queen and she had a glimmer of understanding of how easy it was to slide into such a state and how difficult it must be to get out of it.

Together, she and Violet washed and undressed Marilyn, put her in one of the Queen's own nightgowns, covered the sofa in white linen and prepared for the baby's arrival. The porcelain bowl was filled with boiling water, the baby's layette was put by the gas fire to warm, and the daft teenager was ordered to make tea – using the Queen's own Doulton cups and saucers.

'Break them cups an' I'll break your cowin' neck!' Violet threatened the sullen youth.

The Queen began to line a shallow cardboard box with towels and pillow cases brought from home. 'It's like playing dollies again,' she said to Violet. 'I'm rather enjoying myself.'

'We'll 'ave to clean this shit 'ole up when Marilyn's bin took to the 'ospital. Poor cow shoulda *said*. We'd 'a' 'elped 'er out. Done her washin', got stuff in for the baby, cleaned up.'

'I think she's been too depressed to help herself, don't you?' said the Queen. 'I know somebody in a similar situation.'

'I'm writin' to my MP about this bleedin' ambulance,' said Violet, as she checked to see if the baby's head was visible. 'I'll find out who 'e is an' I'll write to 'im. This is disgusting, I'm too old for this mullarkey.'

Yet her hands were assured as she manipulated Marilyn's body and the Queen was impressed by how readily Marilyn followed Violet's instructions as she told her when to push and when to stop.

'Did you train as a nurse, Violet?' asked the Queen, as she sterilised the scissors in the flames of the gas fire.

'No, you di'n't train for nowt in our family. I passed for a scholarship but there weren't no chance of goin' to grammar school.' Violet laughed at the thought of it. 'Couldn't afford the uniform, an' anyway I 'ad to bring money into the 'ouse.'

'How very unfair,' said the Queen. Marilyn shouted, 'Oh Violet, it's 'orrible, it's 'urtin' me.'

Violet wiped Marilyn's face with a snow-white monogrammed face cloth, then peered between her thighs and said, 'I can see its 'ead, it'll be 'ere soon, you'll soon have your little 'un in your arms.'

Leslie Kerry Violet Elizabeth Monk was born at 2.10 am and weighed five pounds and six ounces. ''Ardly more than a bag a' spuds,' said Violet as she prepared to cut the cord which tied mother to child.

The Queen was entranced by the baby, which lay on Marilyn's belly like a pink pebble on a white beach. Violet asked the Queen to wrap the baby and to clean its face. When this was done, the child opened its lids and looked at the Queen with eyes the colour of sapphires, like those in the brooch her parents gave her when Charles was born.

The Queen gave Leslie to Marilyn, who was babbling with happiness, thankful that the pain had stopped and that her baby wasn't 'deformed or owt like that'. The daft teenager was praised extravagantly because he made more tea without being asked. Leslie was placed in her cardboard box cradle while the women sipped at the orange liquid.

The daft teenager opened the door and three small children dressed in grubby tee-shirts and pants followed him into the room. 'They want to see the baby,' he said. 'You woke 'em up screamin'.'

'It's a girl,' said Marilyn to her common-law stepchildren. 'I've called her Leslie after your dad.' The Queen washed their hands and faces. Then they were allowed to take it in turns to hold the baby. She then led them upstairs and tucked them in under the ragged covers of their shared double bed.

On the landing, she saw her own face: a page torn from a newspaper and stuck to the wall with Christmas sellotape. The photograph showed her in her full regalia – about to open Parliament. The Queen did a quick tour of the bedrooms and bathroom. The stench of poverty and hopelessness filled her nose and mouth and attached itself to her clothing like a slimy skin. 'I expect one gets used to the smell after a while,' thought the Queen as she went downstairs to open the door to the apologetic ambulance man who had finally found Hell Close.

Marilyn and Leslie were put into a carrying chair and humped into the ambulance. Queen Victoria's layette was on Marilyn's lap, inside a Woolworths carrier bag.

'Don't you dare leave this 'ouse,' Violet said to the daft teenager, who was planning to do just that. 'No sneaking off to one of them acid house parties and leavin' them little kids on their own. We'll be round in the mornin', make sure you're in.' He nodded without enthusiasm and went to his own chaotic bed.

Violet wrapped the afterbirth in newspaper, in the manner of an efficient butcher's assistant wrapping a large order of ox liver. Then, in ceremonial manner, she and the Queen went into the back garden where they built a little bonfire and set fire to the meaty parcel. They watched and talked quietly until the afterbirth had been eaten by the flames.

The Queen had rarely felt so close to anyone before. There was something about the firelight which invited swapped confidences. Violet was vulgar and had appalling taste in clothes, but there was an inner strength to her that the Queen admired, even envied. The two women talked about the anguish their children had caused them. The Queen confessed to Violet that, since moving to Hell Close, she had heard nothing from her sons, Andrew and Edward, both of whom were abroad. 'I'm awfully worried,' she said.

Violet snorted. 'Selfish bleeders! They'll soon come running when they want something.'

'I thought,' said the Queen, 'that when they were eighteen they would be off my mind, if not off my hands.'

'Some cowin' chance,' said Violet.

The Queen and Violet poked the embers until they died. Bubble, bubble, toil and trouble, thought the Queen.

When she got home, she looked around at her tidy and clean little house and was grateful for its comfort. And if I'm ever seriously incapacitated, she thought, Violet Toby will help me out.

The Queen went to sleep and dreamt that she was presenting the OBE to Violet, for Services to Humanity.

17 The Briefcase Was Bare

The Queen was eating cornflakes in front of the television. A single cornflake fell from her mouth and landed on the carpet, Harris immediately licked it up.

The Queen said, 'What an absolute *slob* I'm becoming, Harris.' Her attention was then taken by a shouting match that had erupted in the TV-am studio. Jack Barker and the (usually genial) presenter of the programme were arguing about the health of the pound.

The presenter said, 'But, Mr Barker, the pound is desperately weak. It fell a long way last night.' She fixed him with a beady glance.

Really, thought the Queen. She makes it sound as though the pound had attempted a suicide jump from a tall building.

Jack smiled reassuringly: 'But, thanks to the measures we have taken, the pound is now rallying and is expected to hold its own.'

The Queen imagined the pound languishing in a hospital bed hooked up to monitors and drips, surrounded by anxious doctors and financial advisers.

The presenter turned to the camera and said, 'And now, the weather,' and the Queen went into the kitchen to wash her bowl and spoon.

Later that morning, there was a violent row in the street between Violet Toby and Beverley Threadgold.

Beverley wanted to know why she hadn't been woken up to officiate at her sister's confinement. Horrible wounding words were exchanged between the two women. Violet accused Beverley of neglecting Marilyn during her pregnancy. 'When was the last time you were inside your sister's stinking house?' bellowed Violet.

The Queen stood behind her closed front door and listened to the row. Both antagonists were shouting from their respective front gates. It wasn't difficult to hear what they were saying, both had foghorn voices when roused. Residents of Hell Close came out of their houses to enjoy the confrontation – it was unusual to have a shouting match in the spring. The long summer holiday was the traditional time – when the days were hot and the kids fell out and the mothers were irritable and longing for the first day of term.

To her alarm, the Queen heard her name mentioned. Beverley shouted, 'You just wanted to get in with the Queen.'

Violet shouted, 'I ain't no snob. I chose 'er because she were awake an' she don't panic. *Unlike* you, Beverley Threadgold, 'oo can't stand the sight of blood!'

The Queen came away from the door, not wishing to hear any more references to herself. It was true, she did keep a tight grip on herself. Would she go to her grave without experiencing an emotional breakdown? Was it better for one to hang onto the dictates of one's upbringing: good manners, control and self-discipline, or to behave how one *felt* and scream in the street like a demented harridan?

Once, when she was thirteen, she had belched at a dinner for the Hungarian Ambassador – an audible belch that was diplomatically ignored by the other distinguished diners. She had dismissed the belch to Crawfie, saying, 'Oh well, it's better out than in.'

Crawfie had said, 'No, no, no, Lilibet, it is always, always better *in* than out.'

What must it feel like to open one's mouth and *scream*? The Queen stood over the washing-up bowl and gave a tiny, experimental scream. To her ears, it sounded like a hinge needing oil. She tried again. 'Aaaaargh!' Quite satisfactory. And again, 'Aaaaaaaarggh!!!!' Her throat opened wide and the Queen could feel the scream travel up her lungs, overflow her windpipe and roar out of her mouth like a British lion. The scream woke Philip, it brought people running to the Queen's front door. It caused Harris to lie low and flatten his ears, birds left the Queen's garden in a flapping panic, earthworms burrowed deeper.

The scream drew attention away from the row in the street and the man from the Department of Social Security paused before opening the Queen's gate and walking up the path. What on earth was going on *now*? Was the Queen being murdered? Had he brought the correct forms for a Funeral Claim?

The Queen opened the front door and assured her neighbours that she was perfectly well. She had trodden on a drawing pin in her stockinged feet. All eyes looked down. The Queen was wearing sturdy green wellingtons. The man from the DSS pushed through the sceptical crowd and introduced himself: 'I'm David Dorkin, from the DSS. I've come to sort out your benefit.'

The Queen led him into the living room and invited him to sit on the Napoleonic sofa. She advised him to avoid the join where the six inch nails had been hammered in. Dorkin opened his metal briefcase and started to take out his forms and lay them on the lid. He was nervous: who wouldn't be? He couldn't find his pen, and the Queen went to her desk and handed him a heavy gold fountain pen, worth twice his annual salary. Dorkin said, 'I can't use a fountain pen!' He had taken the top off and seen the encrustation of small jewels around the nib. It was too much of a responsibility, he felt. What if he damaged it? There could be a huge insurance claim. He handed the pen back to the Queen, took a deep breath, searched in his beige anorak and located his own rollerball. With a pen in his hand he felt more in command of himself. He declined coffee.

'I'd like your husband to be present at this interview,' said Dorkin.

'My husband is unwell,' said the Queen. 'He has been unwell since we moved in.'

'Since your relocation?' said Dorkin.

'Since we *moved in*,' repeated the Queen.

The rollerball rolled over the page of Dorkin's reporter's notebook.

'And what is the current situation regarding your personal finances?'

'We are penniless. I have been forced to borrow from

my mother; but now my mother is also penniless. As is my entire family. I have been forced to rely on the charity of neighbours. But I cannot continue to do so. My neighbours are. . . .' The Queen paused.

'Socially disadvantaged?' supplied Dorkin.

'No, they are *poor*,' said the Queen. 'They, like me, lack money. I would like you, Mr Dorkin, to give me some money – today, please. I have no food, no heat and when the electricity goes, I will have no light.'

'When your claim is processed and approved, you will receive a giro through the post,' said Dorkin.

As it was Friday the Queen had expected this young man with the prominent adam's apple simply to take banknotes from out of his briefcase and hand them over to her. All of her family were under a similar misapprehension, which was why they had been spending that week with such abandon. She tried once again to explain to Dorkin that she needed the money immediately; there was nothing in the refrigerator, the cupboards were bare.

Right on cue, Prince Philip shuffled into the room, bleating that he'd had no breakfast, demanding to know where his contact lenses were, complaining of the cold.

Dorkin was shocked at Philip's disintegration: seen on television before the election, he had appeared to be a vigorous man, immaculately dressed, with a healthy pink complexion and an arrogant bearing. Dorkin could hardly bring himself to look at the broken wreck in front of him. It was like finding your own father lying drunk in a gutter. The Queen pacified Philip with the promise of coffee, led him to the foot of the stairs and urged him back to bed.

When she re-entered the living room, she saw that David Dorkin had started to fill in a form. Was this the previously-mentioned Claim Form? If so, it must be completed at once. Philip and Harris must be fed. She had always had a small appetite; she would manage. But the man and the dog were helpless and entirely dependent upon her ability to navigate a course through the murky waters of the DSS.

When the form was completed, the Queen asked when she would receive the giro. 'It could be a week, though we're short-staffed, so. . . .' Dorkin's voice trailed off.

'So?'

'It could be longer; perhaps nine, ten days.'

'But how can we exist without food for ten days? You surely won't allow us to *starve*?' said the Queen to the young man. Dorkin grudgingly admitted that starvation was not official policy. 'There is,' he said, 'such a thing as an Emergency Payment.'

'And how does one procure an Emergency Payment?' asked the Queen.

'You have to go to the DSS office, in person,' he said. He warned her that even as he spoke the queue would be out of the door, but the Queen already had her coat on. She simply couldn't keep borrowing from the neighbours. She tied a headscarf around her head. As she had no money, she would have to walk into town.

18 The Gamblers

Fitzroy Toussaint was surprised to find that his mother was not at home. He always called on Fridays at 1 pm and she was usually on the doorstep, waiting for him – whatever the weather. He let himself into her bungalow with a key. Fitzroy was grateful he didn't have to live in the Close himself any more. Once he had taken his 'A' levels he had got the hell out and gone to live in the suburbs. Christ, it was cold! He went through the narrow hall to the kitchen. Good, at least she had plenty of food; the shelves in her high cupboard were well stocked. So why was she so *thin*? She was wasting away, her legs and arms were like sticks, no, twigs.

As usual, the interior of the bungalow was immaculate, the dishcloth was folded into a square on the draining board. He looked into the bedroom and saw that the bed was made and that she had started to knit her Christmas presents for the grandchildren. He was cheered by this – her arthritis couldn't be any worse. He put his head around the living room door and saw a note tucked into the mirror over the cold fireplace.

'Fitzroy, I am next door, with the Queen Mother. Call round, she don't mind, I axed.'

The Queen Mother's door was slightly ajar. Fitzroy pushed it and was met by a gust of hot air. He waited and heard his mother's voice raised in indignation, telling one of her family stories.

'That woman was *evil*, I tell you, to run off and leave her children. . . .'

He heard the Queen Mother's voice trying, and eventually succeeding in cutting in. 'Wallis Simpson was evil too, I'm convinced of it. I will never forgive her for what she did to poor David. It was a dreadful time for us all. Abdication! It was so shaming. He knew my husband, George didn't want to be King – who would, with a stammer like his? All those speeches, it was torture for him – and me.'

Fitzroy heard his mother shouting the Queen Mother down. 'An' this is another wicked woman! Me Aunt Matilda. Man, that woman was crazy for the drink. See, if you look careful you can see the bottle in her hand.'

Fitzroy knocked on the living room door, walked in and found two old ladies, each looking through her own family photograph album. Both too old to care what other people thought of them, both relishing the airing of family secrets.

Fitzroy saw the pleasure on his mother's face when she saw him. He also saw the slight flicker of fear on the Queen Mother's face. Did she think he was going to rob her? Did the suit and the Filofax he was carrying under his arm count for nothing?

'Hello Mum,' he said, and was only a little surprised when both women said, 'Hello, Fitzroy.'

His mother bombarded him with questions as usual. How was his chest? Was he still working hard? Was he cooking himself proper meals? Had he heard from

Troy? Why had he shaved off his moustache? It was cold, was he wearing a vest? Had he visited Jethroe's grave? Did he want a hot drink?

The Queen Mother insisted that they must take tea with her. She got up from her chair with great difficulty, Fitzroy noticed. He offered her his hand and she leaned heavily against him.

'Sit down, woman!' shouted Philomena. 'Talk to me son. I hain't as old as you. I'll make the tea.'

She stomped off into the kitchen as though it were her own house. The Queen Mother sat down and asked Fitzroy if he was interested in horses. Fitzroy wondered if this was a trap. He had promised his mother that he would never gamble. On his eighteenth birthday she had made him swear on the Bible that he would never set foot inside a bookie's shop. He had kept his promise.

When he was twenty-one, he had opened a telephone account with Jack Johnson, Turf Accountant. His winnings were sent straight into his bank account but, like the Queen Mother, he had never set foot inside a bookie's shop. He lowered his voice and moved nearer to the Queen Mother.

'Yeah, I'm interested.'

'In form?'

'Yeah, in form.'

'Who trained my grandson's horse, Sea Swell?' Fitzroy answered at once, 'Nick Gaselee, for the Duke of Gloucester Memorial Trophy. Prince Charles finished fourth.'

'Yes, I lost twenty-five pounds.'

The Queen Mother pulled from her corsage a

five pound note she had been concealing from her daughter and handed it to Fitzroy.

'Sea Mist – Kempton Park, two o'clock,' she said, with her eye on the kitchen door.

'To win?'

'Oh yes, it's a cert, the going's soft, he likes it soft.'

Fitzroy took a mobile telephone from the inside pocket of his Paul Smith jacket. He pressed the buttons and placed the Queen Mother's bet. And, just to be friendly, he put twenty-five pounds on Sea Mist himself. They swapped gambling stories until Philomena came in with the tea tray and they talked about Fitzroy's job. He was an insolvency accountant, currently bringing a chain of shoe shops to a peaceful end. He promised to get the Queen Mother a pair of wide-fitting brocade house slippers – at a discount.

At 2.15 Fitzroy's telephone rang. Philomena was washing up noisily in the kitchen. 'Yeah?' he said, looking at the Queen Mother. 'Wellwotjano! You've won yourself a tidy amount.'

The Queen Mother's eyes glittered greedily.

'Right,' she whispered. 'Nectarine – Kempton Park; two-thirty. Twenty pounds each way.'

It made him late getting back to the office but he waited until 2.35, when the phone rang again. This time his mother was back in the room so all he did was show the Queen Mother his downturned thumb. She understood at once.

Philomena collected up her photograph albums and ordered the Queen Mother to have a nap. She was tired herself and needed to sleep.

Fitzroy saw his mother to her front door and handed

her a small plastic bag full of fifty pence coins. 'For the gas meter,' he said. 'Use them.' He walked to his Ford Sierra with an extra spring in his step, pleased with his winnings and glad that his mother had a friend. Man, it took a weight off his shoulders. He pressed a button on his key ring and a mysterious electronic process caused the door locks to pop up in unison. He waved goodbye to the two old ladies waving from their respective front windows and reversed towards the barrier. He didn't like meeting the police head on. Never had.

19 The Long Walk

Harris was playing in the street with the Pack. The Queen stood on her doorstep calling him in, but he refused to come. She ran out into the street, shouting his name angrily. A gang of children joined in the chase. What a scruffy bunch they were, thought the Queen. Then she noticed that running amongst them, like feral animals, were her own grandchildren, William and Harry. Harris ran and hid under a wrecked and burnt out Renault car that stood at the kerb. The Queen lured him out with a polo mint she'd found in the pocket of her waxed coat, then she thrashed him with his lead. But it was a gentle thrashing.

Harris allowed the lead to be slipped over his head and the Queen set off to walk the three miles into town. As she approached the barrier, she saw that PC Ludlow was on duty, checking the licence of a handsome and smartly dressed black man who was behind the wheel of a Ford Sierra.

When the car had reversed rapidly out of Hell Close, she went up to Ludlow and demanded to know why he had told such shocking lies in court. PC Ludlow had dreaded this moment. He hadn't slept properly for three nights – guilt had kept him awake. He had listened to the World Service on his clock radio until the early hours, trying to blot out the memory of the crime he had committed. Perjury was a serious offence; he could lose his job. It was unlikely, but you never knew nowadays.

Inspector Holyland had told him what to say and he had said it, word for word. He hadn't expected to be believed. 'Kill the pig!' He had expected the magistrates and the court and the public gallery to burst into laughter at the thought of the Prince of Wales uttering these clichéd words, but he was wearing his uniform, he represented Law and Order and Truth; and Inspector Holyland had backed him up, although he hadn't been on the scene at the time.

The Queen repeated, 'Why did you tell those lies about my son?' Ludlow said, 'Those were the facts as I saw them, at the time.' Harris was sniffing around the bottom of his trousers. Ludlow moved his feet and Harris, interpreting this as an aggressive gesture, sank his teeth into a regulation police sock, piercing the skin below. In Ludlow's opinion, the Queen took an unnecessarily long time in pulling Harris away from his left ankle. There was a form to fill in before she was allowed to leave Hell Close.

Name	Elizabeth Windsor
Address	9 Hell Close
Time	2.45 pm
Destination	DSS Middleton
Method of Transport	Walking
Estimated time of return	6 pm

Ludlow lifted the barrier and she walked through.

A bogus beast followed her, keeping his distance.

Surely she wasn't going to *walk* into town? He'd got new shoes on. His feet would be in tatters. He was festooned in corn plasters as it was. He was sick of being in plain clothes. He longed for the comfort of his old panda car. His name was Colin Lightfoot, his duty was to shadow the Queen and report back to Inspector Holyland.

The Queen was quite enjoying the walk, though she would have preferred to be on Holkham Beach, near Sandringham – or striding through the heather at Balmoral. But at least she was out of Hell Close and getting some exercise. Harris hated it. The pavements were hard on his feet and his little legs could hardly keep up with the Queen's vigorous pace.

They were walking alongside the dual carriageway that connected the Flowers Estate to the town. The Queen had visited the town before; she had opened a hospital, visited a hosiery and light engineering factory in the morning and, after lunch in the Town Hall, had visited an institution for the elderly confused in the afternoon, where she had made excruciatingly embarrassing conversation with the residents. One old, dribbling man was convinced that she was his mother and that it was 1941 and that he was still in the Catering Corps. On her way back to the Royal Train, she had called in at a probation hostel where she was given a tour of the gleaming dormitories and the freshly-painted ping-pong room. A few presentable probationers had been allowed to look on while the daughter of the Director of Social Services had given her a bunch of spring flowers. She wondered now where the other, probably less presentable, probationers had been kept.

It began to rain; a steady remorseless sheet of water. She pulled her headscarf lower, over her forehead, and strode on. The bogus beast behind her cursed and swore and shook his fist at the heavens and, as if to taunt him, a police car drove by, the uniformed occupants looking warm and smug as they conveyed Mr Christmas to Tulip Street Police Station.

She looked at her watch and quickened her step. Mr Dorkin had told her that the office closed at 5.30. He had written down the address on a sheet of paper. The Queen took the folded sheet from her pocket. The only legible words were 'DSS Office'. The remaining address was completely illegible, rain had run into her pocket and obliterated everything below the fold of the paper.

Harris tried to match the Queen's more urgent pace to his own, but after a few minutes he had had enough and refused to go on. He *knew* he should have worn his raincoat. He had stood under the coat rack in the hall. He had barked and indicated that he would like to be strapped into his little coat, but *she* was in too much of a hurry to notice *him*, wasn't she? Oh yes, hadn't got a moment now to feed him and tell him that he was her favourite. And what *was* it with all this physical *violence*? A beating a day – at least. If she wasn't careful . . . he knew about the RSPCA. And, another thing, he had *serious* fleas. The Queen yanked on Harris's lead, but he refused to budge. She tried dragging him along but he sat down and dug his paws in. A bedraggled passer-by said, 'You'll have the skin off that dog's arse.'

The Queen replied, 'I'll have the skin off that dog's *back* if he doesn't move.' She pushed Harris with her foot and he yelped as though in agony and lay on his back feigning death. Through a slit in one eye, he watched as the Queen bent over him, her eyes full of concern and guilt. He felt himself being lifted up and cradled in her arms.

Their journey continued along the dual carriageway towards the town where the pavements were not paved with gold – they were hardly paved at all. The Council were investing their money in buying a windswept thousand-acre site on the outskirts of the town where they planned to build a theme park: a zoo without animals. Instead of the mess and the smell and the necessity to feed real wild animals, the Council had been persuaded by a private company to build a series of huge windowless edifices. Inside, electronic imagery and sophisticated sound systems were to replicate the continents of the world and their indigenous animals. It was Virtual Reality on a huge scale. Millions of goggling visitors were expected to visit the windswept site from all over Britain. A five hundred bed hotel was to be built to accommodate them. The narrow minor roads leading to the site were to be widened slightly. They had hoped that Prince Philip (in his capacity as President of the World Wildlife Fund, rather than his other well-known role as killer of small birds and animals) would open the electronic zoo for them.

When the Queen reached the town centre, she rested on a bench and put Harris on his feet. He lifted his leg and urinated against an overflowing litter bin. The Queen was reminded of Niagara Falls, the flow of which, unlike Harris, could be switched off at will.

A man was sitting next to the Queen. He had a raw, recently broken nose. He was drinking out of a brown bottle. After each drink he drew a filthy hand across his mouth, as if hiding the evidence. His shoes were of the type worn by bandleaders between the wars. Harris's urine trickled towards these shoes and the man drew his feet onto the bench in a decorous movement, like a young girl avoiding a strolling spider.

The Queen apologised for Harris's behaviour.

'Och, the wee dog canna help it,' said the man, his voice hoarse from violent shouting in the small hours. 'An' let's face it, missus, he's too wee to climb onto a lavatory seat.'

The man laughed and choked at his joke and when he saw that the Queen was not laughing, he prodded her and said, 'Aw, c'mon, lassie, let yourself go. You've got a face on you like a wet Sunday in Aberdeen.'

The Queen showed her teeth briefly and the man was pacified.

He said, 'D'you know who you look like? I'll tell you. You look like that woman who impersonates the Queen. You do, you do, you look like her – wassaname? You know the one. You look *more* like her than she does. You do. You do. You could make a *fortune*. You shid do it, you shid. You shid do it. You know who *I've* been taken for?'

The Queen looked at his broken veined face. His tropical sunset eyes, his matted hair, his verdigris teeth.

'G'wan, guess who I'm took for?'

'I simply can't imagine,' said the Queen, turning her head away from his cidery breath.

'Hee, hee, hee,' laughed the man. 'Hee, hee, hee, that's verra guid. You sound jus' like her. "*Ai simplay carrnt eemaygin*",' he mocked. 'Jus' like her, jus' like the Queen. You shid go on the clubs, you shid. "*Ai simplay carrnt eemaygin*".' His laughter echoed around the town centre. He beat on his thighs with his fists. 'I mean, you're not tellin' me that her accent is *real*. It's not, it's not. It's not real. She sounds like a robot from *Doctor Who*. Doesn't she, missus? Doesn't she? Still, we're rid of her now. Guid riddance, I say. I'll drink to that. I'll drink to that. Who's in charge now?'

'Jack Barker,' said the Queen, trying to flatten her vowels.

'Tee hee, hee. *Jek Barker*. You're a scream, missus,' said the Republican. 'You are, you are, you are.'

He stood up and swayed in front of the Queen. She noticed that he was not wearing socks. His trouser hems had fallen down; overlocking threads trailed behind him. If ever asked by a style magazine journalist to explain how he chose each day's wardrobe, he would have to say in all honesty that he threw his clothes on in the morning and continued to wear them day and night until many months later when they were removed by men wearing rubber gloves, overalls and face masks.

'G'wan, who do I remind you of?' He struck what he perceived to be an artistic pose. One finger on his chin, and his head turned to display his wrecked profile.

The Queen shook her head; she didn't know.

'The Duke,' shouted the dissolute one. He saw

that the Queen was not familiar with the name. 'Prince Philip. I'm a dead ringer for him; everybody says, everybody. Can you not see it? Can you not?'

The Queen eventually admitted that perhaps there was a 'slight resemblance'. He drank the bottle dry, then shook it and steered two brown drops into his gaping mouth. He shook it again, inverted it against his mouth, waited, got angry when nothing appeared and banged his teeth on the rim.

'You wouldn't have the price of a Big Mac, would you missus?' he asked.

'No,' said the Queen, placing the cider bottle against the litter bin. 'I do not have a penny.'

'Och, that's what they all say, though not in such a classy accent.'

The Queen asked him for directions to the DSS office. He offered to escort the Queen to the door, but she declined graciously. As she waited for the green man to give her permission to cross the road, she heard the grimy one shout, 'Jeanette Charles! That's her, that's her, that's the one. You're a dead ringer for her. A fortune! A fortune!'

The Queen joined the queue outside the DSS office. A girl in unmemorable clothes gave her a numbered disc – thirty-nine. She stood behind number thirty-eight and was soon joined by forty. Those in the queue with watches looked at them, frequently. Those without asked the time, often.

Time, invisible and invincible, fled by, mocking those waiting outside. Would they be seen? There were twenty-five minutes left. They did mathematical calculations inside their heads. Little children stood stoically holding onto the pushchairs of their younger siblings. The rush hour traffic jerked by, three feet away, sending fumes directly into the lungs of the occupants of the pushchairs.

Harris coughed and strained on his lead.

The queue shuffled in until the Queen was sufficiently far forward to be able to see inside the large room where a menacing clock with black hands and a hurrying second hand told her that it was twelve minutes past five. A baby began to cry and was given an unopened packet of crisps to suck.

"S no good givin' him a actual *crisp*, they're salt and vinegar,' said the young mother – number thirty-eight. "E don't like salt 'n' vinegar.'

The Queen nodded, reluctant to open her mouth and advertise her class. Her accent was proving to be rather a bother. Should she try to modify it? And her grammar was a nuisance. Should she throw in a few double negatives? It was terribly difficult to work out where she *belonged* any more – except as a number between thirty-eight and forty.

As the hands of the clock moved towards 5.30, the queue started to panic and surge towards the counters where claimants were seated, pleading their cases through grilles set into sheets of safety glass.

Words of supplication, anger and desperation passed one way through the screen from the waiting room to the office. In the other direction passed words pertaining to regulations, explanations and refusal. A man stood up and banged on the screen, 'I need some money – now,' he shouted. 'I can't go home without some money. We've got nowt.'

The clerk sat impassively and watched a security guard lead the man away.

'Thirty-six,' said the clerk. 'Thirty-seven,' said another.

A third clerk left her desk and gathered her papers and her boxed pen and pencil set together. She slung the strap of her bag over her shoulder and prepared to leave.

The Queen left her place in the queue and said through the grille, 'Excuse me, but at what time do you leave your work?'

The clerk said reluctantly, 'Half past five.'

'Then you have five minutes left,' said the Queen. 'Perhaps your watch is rather fast.'

The clerk resumed her seat and said, 'Thirty-eight.' The Queen rejoined the queue, who were pleased at the small victory. Behind her, forty said, 'Good show, ma'am.' He came closer and said out of the side of his mouth, 'I had the honour to serve in your regiment, Welsh Guards. Saw action in the Falklands, Bluff Cove. Honourable discharge. Nerves gone to pot.'

'A bad show,' said the Queen, who was the former Colonel-in-Chief of thirty-eight regiments and the Captain General of seven others.

Her number was called by a pleasant-looking Asian youth. The Queen had two minutes in which to state her case and leave with bus fare, food money and coins for the meters. 'It's impossible,' smiled the youth, after she had answered that no, she had no documentation to prove who she was and where she lived.

'To get an Emergency Payment, we need proof; a pension book? A gas bill?'

The Queen explained that she had not yet received her pension book. She had only been in her present accommodation for four days.

'And where did you live before?' asked the youth.

'At Buckingham Palace,' answered the Queen.

'Sure you did,' laughed the youth, looking at the Queen's coat covered in muddy paw prints, at her grimy nails, her wet straggling hair. Honest. He had heard all sorts of stories. He could write a book! Two books. Honest.

'And why were you living in Buckingham Palace?' he asked, raising his voice so that his fellow workers would be able to share the joke.

'Because I was the Queen,' said the Queen.

The youth pressed a buzzer under his counter and a security guard took the Queen's arm and led her and Harris out into the dark evening. She stood on the pavement, not knowing what to do or where to go for help. She tried all her pockets, searching for a coin for the telephone, though she knew perfectly well that her pockets were completely empty apart from a sheet of lavatory paper torn from a roll. She didn't know that it was possible to make a reverse charge call through the operator.

It was Friday night, the DSS would be closed for two days. They had money, she had none.

Dragging Harris behind her, she ran back into the office. The staff were wearing their coats. The clock said that it was five twenty-nine and thirty seconds. Claimants were being escorted from the room. The Queen noticed that number thirty-eight had a five pound note in her hand and was talking to her baby:

telling the child that she was going to buy milk and bread and nappies. Forty was refusing to leave, 'I was at Bluff Cove,' he was shouting.

The Queen picked Harris up and put him under her arm. 'My dog is starving,' she announced to the room.

Clerk number two lived with her mother, three dogs and five cats. She had wanted to be a vet but couldn't get the 'A' levels. She looked at Harris, who lay languidly in the Queen's arms as though he were in the last stages of malnutrition. The clerk sat down behind her desk. She unbuttoned her coat, reached for a pen and invited the Queen to sit down. First she lectured the Queen on the responsibilities of dog ownership, saying, 'You shouldn't really keep a dog unless you're prepared to, well, *keep* it properly.'

Harris whimpered pitifully and allowed his ears to droop. The clerk continued her lecture. 'He looks in very bad condition. I'm going to give you enough for a couple of tins of dog food and some conditioning tablets – Bob Martin's are good.'

The Queen took the money, signed the receipt and left the office. She thanked God that the English were a nation of dog lovers.

20 A Bag of Bones

The bogus beast followed her. As she left the office, he prayed that she was not planning to walk home. His feet were raw lumps of meat. He couldn't wait to take his shoes off. The Queen clutched the three pound coins tightly in her hand. How much was a loaf of bread? A pound of potatoes? A jar of coffee? She had no intention of buying dog food or conditioning tablets for Harris.

Crawfie used to make broth whenever the Queen was ill as a child. The Queen remembered that bones were involved. She passed a butcher's shop. A man in a white coat and striped apron was scrubbing the shelves in the display cabinet. Small bunches of plastic parsley were piled up on the shop counter, waiting to be replaced in order to beautify the shelves. The Queen tied Harris up outside and pushed the door open.

'We're closed,' said the butcher.

'Could you sell me some bones?' asked the Queen.

'I'm closed,' he said.

The Queen pleaded, 'Please. They're for my dog.'

The butcher sighed, went out to the back and returned with a collection of gruesome bones which he slung on to the scales.

'Thirty pence,' he said, brusquely, wrapping them loosely in a sheet of paper. The Queen handed him a pound coin and he took the change from a bag of coins and handed it to her without a smile.

'May I have a carrier bag?' the Queen asked.

'No, not for thirty pence,' said the butcher.

'Oh well, thank you and goodnight,' said the Queen. She didn't know how much it would cost to buy a carrier. She couldn't risk spending perhaps twenty or thirty pence more.

The Queen said again, 'Goodnight.'

The butcher turned his back and began to place the plastic parsley around the edge of the display shelves.

The Queen said, 'Have I offended you in some way?'

The butcher said, 'Look, you've got your thirty pence worth, just close the door behind you.'

Before she could do as she was told, a well-dressed man came into the shop and said, 'I can see you're closed, but will you sell me three pounds of fillet steak?'

The butcher smiled and said, 'Certainly, sir, won't be a tick.'

The Queen took her bones and left. As she untied Harris, she watched the butcher through the window as he sliced fat slices of steak from a large lump of beef. He was now all jollity, like a butcher on a playing card.

Harris was maddened by the smell of the bones. He leapt up toward the parcel which was tucked under the Queen's arm. When they got to the bus stop, she threw a small knuckle bone onto the pavement and he attacked it ferociously; holding it in his front paws and tearing at the wisps of flesh with guttural, greedy sounds.

The bone was stripped bare by the time the bus arrived. The town centre was almost deserted. The Queen dreaded the weekend ahead. How did one feed oneself, one's husband and one's dog on two pounds and ten pence, which was all she had, after paying her bus fare? She simply could not borrow any more. She would pray that her pension book came in the post tomorrow.

The Queen said, 'One to the Flowers Estate, please.'

She put sixty pence in the driver's black scoop bowl and waited for her ticket. The driver said, 'I want ninety pee. It's 'alf fare for the dog.'

The Queen was horrified, 'Surely not?'

'Dog's 'alf fare,' repeated the driver.

The Queen gave Harris a venomous look. For two pins, she'd make him run behind the bus. He'd been nothing but a nuisance all day. However, she paid up and, as instructed by the driver, carried Harris upstairs to the top deck. She counted and recounted her money, but always came to the same total: one pound and eighty pence. She closed her eyes and prayed for a miracle – of the loaves and fishes variety.

The Queen got off the bus and went into the Food-U-R – the supermarket that served the Flowers Estate. The manager and owner was Victor Berryman. He stood at the door greeting customers and watching out for shoplifters.

'Evening, madam. Settling in all right?'

The Queen smiled and nodded. 'Yes, finding one's way.'

'That's what I like to hear. Sorry to hear about your husband.'

'My husband?'

'Yes, I hear he's bad.'

'Bad?'

'Poorly, off his head.'

'He's depressed, certainly.'

'I know how he feels. I used to have a chain of these, you know. There were Food-U-Rs all over the East Midlands. Adverts on the telly. The hula girls? Food-U-R – a Paradise for Shoppers?' He sang the jingle and swayed his bulky hips.

Food-U-R!
A Paradise for Shoppers.
Food-U-R!

'I tried to get the girls to go with the Polynesian theme – you know, grass skirts, garlands, but there was nothing but complaints.'

He looked bitterly towards the checkouts where two dumpy, middle-aged women were passing groceries in front of electronic scanners: 'Yes, I was once head of a dynasty, so I know how your husband feels – having it snatched away.'

The Queen scowled.'My husband was not the head of the dynasty. I was.'

Victor Berryman snatched a Mars Bar from the inside jacket pocket of a departing boy, clipped him round the ear and kicked him out of the shop.

'Anyway, madam, if there's anything I can do to help,' said Victor, shaking his fist at the boy.

The Queen explained that she wished to make a broth.

'A brawth?' repeated Victor.

'A broth – a thin stew,' the Queen explained. 'I have the bones, what else does one need?'

Victor looked baffled, the kitchen was a place of mystery to him. All he knew was that cold ingredients were taken in and hot food came out, at more or less regular intervals. He called to one of the women at the checkout, 'Mrs Maundy, help this lady out, will you? I'll take over the till.'

Mrs Maundy gave the Queen a half curtsey and a wire basket and they promenaded up and down the aisles. The Queen bought one onion, two carrots, one turnip, one pound of potatoes, a large loaf of bread, a jar of strawberry jam (small) and two Oxo cubes.

Victor Berryman passed the Queen's groceries over the magic eye and said, 'One pound fifty-eight pence.'

'Oh dear.'

The Queen looked at the pound and eighty pence in her hand.

'I will have to put something back,' she said. 'I need fifty pence for the meter.'

Between them, they worked out that if she discarded one carrot and one Oxo cube, and swapped a large loaf for a small one. . . .

The Queen left the shop carrying a Food-U-R bag. Victor held the door open for her and said he hoped he would see her again, perhaps she would recommend him to her family and, if she had a spare crest hanging around doing nothing, he'd be pleased to hang it up over the front door.

The Queen had been trained to ask questions, so, as she untied Harris's lead from a concrete bollard, she asked Victor how he had lost his dynasty of Food-U-R stores.

'The Bank,' he answered as he checked the padlocks on the metal grilles that covered the windows. 'They hassled me to borrow money to expand. Then interest rates went up an' I couldn't make the payments. Serves me right, really, I lost the lot. The wife took it hard; house was sold, cars. Nobody wanted to buy this place on the Flowers Estate – who would, 'part from a maniac? We live above the shop now.' The Queen looked up and saw a woman whom she took to be Mrs Berryman, looking sadly out of an uncurtained window.

'Still,' said Victor, 'it's nothing to what *you've* lost, is it?'

The Queen, who had lost palaces, property, land, jewels, paintings, houses, a yacht, a plane, a train, over a thousand servants and billions of pounds, nodded her agreement.

Victor took out a comb and drew it across his bald head. 'Next time you're here, come up and see the wife. Have a cup of tea – she's always in; she's an agoraphobic.' The Queen looked up again, but the sad face at the window had gone.

Clutching her fifty pence coin in her hand, the Queen walked back to Hell Close. Behind her, keeping his distance, limped the bogus beast. If this is plain clothes duty, give me a uniform any day, he thought.

As the Queen let herself into her house, she heard a familiar cough. Margaret was there. Yes, there she sat, smoking and tapping ash into a coffee cup.

'Lilibet, you look absolutely ghastly! And what have you got in that horrid smelly plastic bag?'

'Bones, for our dinner.'

Margaret said: 'I've had the most appalling time this afternoon with a ghastly little man from the Social Security. He was unspeakably vile.'

They moved into the kitchen. The Queen half-filled a saucepan with water and threw the bones into it. Margaret watched intently as though the Queen were Paul Daniels about to perform a magic trick.

'Are you good at peeling potatoes, Margaret?'

'No, of course not, are you?'

'No, but one has to try.'

'Go ahead, try,' yawned Margaret. 'I'm going out to dinner tonight. I telephoned Bobo Criche-Hutchinson, he's got a house in the county. He's picking me up at 8.30.'

A scum formed on the saucepan, then the water boiled over and extinguished the gas flame. The Queen relit the gas ring and said, 'You know we aren't allowed to go out to dinner; we're still under curfew. You'd better ring Bobo and put him off. You haven't read Jack Barker's sheet of instructions, have you?'

'No, I tore it into pieces.'

'Better read mine,' said the Queen, as she hacked at a King Edward with a table knife. 'In my handbag.'

When she had finished reading, Margaret inserted another cigarette inside a holder and said, 'I'll kill myself.'

'That is one option,' said the Queen. 'But what would Crawfie think if you did?'

'Who cares *what* that evil old witch thinks about anything? Anyway, she's dead,' burst out Margaret.

'Not for me, she's not. She's with me at all times, Margaret.'

'She hated me,' said Margaret. 'She made no secret of it.'

'You were a hateful little girl, that's why. Bossy, arrogant and sly,' said the Queen. 'Crawfie said you'd make a mess of your life and she was right – you have.'

After half an hour of silence, the Queen apologised for her outburst. She explained that Hell Close had that effect on one. One got used to speaking one's mind. It was inconvenient at times, but one felt strangely *good* afterwards.

Margaret went into the living room to telephone Bobo Criche-Hutchinson, leaving the Queen to throw the root vegetables and the Oxo cube into the saucepan. Mrs Maundy had told her that broth has to simmer on a low heat for hours – 'to draw the goodness out' – but the Queen was ravenous, she needed to eat *now*, *at once*. Something tasty and filling and sweet. She reached for the bread and jam and made herself a pile of sandwiches. She ate standing at the worktop without a plate or napkin.

She had once been reassured by a senior politician – a woman – that the reason the poor could not manage on their state benefits was because 'they hadn't the aptitude to cook good, simple, nutritious meals.'

The Queen looked at her good, simple, nutritious broth bubbling in the pan and reached for another slice of bread and jam.

That evening, Prince Philip prowled around the bedroom muttering to himself. He stared out of the window. The street teemed with relations. He saw his wife and his sister-in-law coming out of his daughter-in-law's house. They crossed the road leading towards his mother-in-law's bungalow. He could see his son digging the front garden, *in the dark*, the bloody fool! Philip felt trapped by his relations. The buggers were everywhere. Anne, hanging curtains, helped by Peter and Zara. William and Harry yelling from inside a wrecked car. He felt like a beleaguered cowboy in the middle of a wagon train with the bloody Indians closing in.

He got back into bed. The vile broth, now cold, which his wife had earlier brought him, slopped over onto the silver tray and then onto the counterpane. He did nothing to stem the flow. He was too tired. He pulled the sheet over his head and wished himself somewhere else. Anywhere but here.

21 Winging It

The Yeoman Raven Master passed the White Tower, then retraced his steps. Something was wrong, he couldn't put his finger on it immediately. He stood still, the better to think. Japanese tourists took his photograph. A party of German adolescents sniggered at his silly hat. Americans asked if it was really true, that the Queen of England was living on a public housing project.

The Yeoman Raven Master remembered what was wrong at precisely the same time as a schoolgirl from Tokyo pressed the button on her Nikon. When the photograph was developed, it showed the Yeoman Raven Master with his mouth open in horror, his eyes wide with primeval fear.

The Ravens had gone from the Tower: the kingdom would fall.

22 Thin on the Ground

It was Harry's first day at his new school. Marigold Road Junior. Charles stood outside the headmistress's office, wondering whether or not to go in. An argument of some kind was going on inside. He could hear raised female voices, but not what was being said.

Harry said, 'Eh up, Dad, what's goin' on?'

Charles yanked Harry's hand and said: 'Harry, for goodness' sake, speak properly.'

Harry said, 'If I speak proper I get my cowin' face smashed in.'

'By whom?' asked Charles, looking concerned.

'By *who*,' corrected Harry. 'By the kids in 'Ell Close, tha's who.'

Violet Toby came out of the headmistress's office, closely followed by the headmistress, Mrs Strickland.

Violet shouted, 'You lay a finger on one a my grandkids again and I'll 'ave you up, you 'ard-faced cow.'

Mrs Strickland did have rather a *determined* face, thought Charles. He felt the old familiar fear that schools always induced in him. He held even tighter onto Harry's hand – poor little blighter.

Mrs Strickland smiled icily at Charles and said: 'I'm sorry about that unfortunate scene. It was necessary to punish Chantelle Toby on Friday and her grandmother rather took exception to it. Indeed, she seems to have brooded on it over the weekend.'

Charles said, 'Ah! Well, I hope it won't be necessary to punish Harry, he's quite a sensitive little chap.'

'No I ain't,' said Harry.

Charles winced at Harry's ungrammatical protestation and said, 'If you tell me which class Harry is to join, I'll take him along. . . .' A drop of water fell onto Charles's head. He wiped it away and, as he did so, felt another splash onto his hand.

'Oh dear, it's started to rain,' said Mrs Strickland. Charles looked up and saw water splashing down from cracks in the ceiling. A bell rang urgently throughout the school.

'Is that the fire alarm?' asked Charles.

'No, it's the rain alarm,' said Mrs Strickland. 'The bucket monitors will be along soon, excuse me.'

And sure enough, as Charles and Harry watched, children came from all directions and lined up outside Mrs Strickland's office. Mrs Strickland appeared at the door with a heap of plastic buckets which she doled out to the children, who took them and placed them strategically underneath the drips in the corridor. Other buckets were borne away into the classrooms. Charles was impressed with the calm efficiency of the operation. He remarked on it to Mrs Strickland.

'Oh, they're well practised,' she said, rebuffing the compliment. 'We've been waiting for our new roof for five years.'

'Oh dear,' said Charles. 'Er, have you tried fund-raising?'

'Yes,' said Mrs Strickland, bitterly. 'We raised enough money to buy three dozen plastic buckets.'

Harry said in a piercing whisper, 'Dad, I gotta' havva' wee.'

Charles said to Mrs Strickland, 'Where, er, does one take him?'

'Across there,' said Mrs Strickland, pointing to the playground where rain was rapidly filling the potholes. 'He'll need this.'

She reached inside her office door and handed Harry an umbrella, decorated with the vapidly grinning face of Postman Pat.

'No inside lavatories?' said Charles in astonishment.

'No,' said Mrs Strickland.

They watched Harry struggling to open the umbrella before dashing through the rain towards a grim out-building where the lavatories were housed. Charles had offered to accompany his son, but Harry had shouted, 'Don't show me up, our Dad.'

Charles went into the headmistress's office and filled in a form registering Harry at Marigold Street Junior School. He was pleased to be told by Mrs Strickland that Harry qualified for free school dinners. When Harry had handed the dripping umbrella back to Mrs Strickland and she had replaced it in the umbrella stand inside her office, she led them along to Harry's classroom.

'Your teacher is Mr Newman,' she said to Harry.

They reached Mr Newman's classroom and Mrs Strickland knocked and walked in. Nobody saw or heard them enter. The children in the classroom were laughing too loudly at Mr Newman, who was doing a deadly accurate impression of the headmistress. Even Charles, whose acquaintance with Mrs Strickland was brief, could see that Mr Newman was an excellent mimic. He'd captured the jutting jaw, the brusque tones and the stooping posture perfectly. Only when the children fell quiet did Mr Newman turn and see his visitors.

'Ah!' he said to Mrs Strickland. 'You caught me doing my Quasimodo impression: we're doing French literature this morning.'

'*French* literature!' snapped Mrs Strickland. 'Those children have yet to learn any *English* literature.'

'That's because we haven't got any *books*,' said Mr Newman. 'I'm having to photocopy pages out of my own books – at my own expense.'

He bent down and shook Harry's hand, saying, 'I'm Mr Newman, your new teacher, and you're Harry, aren't you? Charmaine, look after Harry for today, will you?'

A plump little girl in gaudy bermuda shorts and a Terminator Two tee-shirt came to the front of the class and pulled Harry away from his father and towards a vacant chair next to her own.

'He's a free school dinner child!' announced Mrs Strickland, loudly. Mr Newman said quietly, 'They're *all* free school dinner children; he's among friends.'

Charles waved to Harry and left with Mrs Strickland. As they wove a path through the buckets in the corridor, Charles said, 'So, you're short of books, are you?'

'And paper and pencils and glue and paint and gym equipment and cutlery for the dining room and *staff*,' said Mrs Strickland. 'But apart from all that we're a very well equipped school.' She added, 'Our parents are very supportive, but they haven't any money. There is a limit to how many raffle tickets they can buy and car boot sales they can attend. These are not the leafy suburbs, Mr Teck.'

Charles agreed; leaves were very thin on the ground on the Flowers Estate – even in autumn, he suspected.

May

23 Peas in a Pod

It was May Day. Charles shouted to Diana: 'Darling, close your eyes. I've got a surprise.'

Diana, who hadn't yet *opened* her eyes – it was only 6.30 in the morning, for goodness' sake – turned over in bed and faced the door. Charles came out of the bathroom and approached the bedside.

'Open your eyes.'

She opened one eye, then the other. He looked the same as ever, perhaps his hair was sleeker than usual. . . . Then Charles turned his back and Diana gasped in dismay. He had a pony tail, only a very tiny one as yet, but even so. . . . A bright red towelling band held his hair together at the nape of his neck. His ears were more prominent than ever.

'You look *fab*, darling.'

'Truly?'

'Yah, fabbo.'

'D'you think Mummy will like it?' Charles's face wrinkled into worry.

'Dunno. Your pa won't.'

'But you do?'

'It's fabuloso.'

'The beetroot is through and we've got our first blackbird sitting on its eggs.'

'Fabulous.'

Diana was getting used to these early morning gardening reports. He was up every morning at six, clumping around the garden in his wellingtons. She had *tried* to show interest, but gracious. . . . She dreaded the autumn when he apparently expected her to preserve and pickle. He had asked her to start collecting empty jars, anticipating a glut of home grown produce. She got out of bed and reached for her silk robe.

'I'm so happy; are you?' he asked.

'Fabulously,' she lied.

'I mean,' said Charles, 'it proves that the garden is ecologically sound. Blackbirds won't. . . .'

They heard Shadow crying through the party wall, followed by the creak of the bed springs as his mother got out of bed to give him his bottle of tea. Before going into the bathroom, Diana asked, 'Charles, I need to have my hair done. Could I have some money?'

Charles said, 'But I was planning to buy a bag of bonemeal this week.'

Through the wall Sharon shouted: 'I'll cut your 'air for you, Di. I used to be 'prentissed to an 'airdresser. Come round at ten.'

Charles said, 'The sound insulation in these houses is appalling. It's well, *non*-existent.'

Through the other party wall Diana and Charles heard Wilf Toby say to his wife, 'I 'ope Diana won't have 'er 'air cut too short.'

They heard the Tobys' headboard bang against the wall as Violet said, 'Oh shut your prattle,' and turned over in bed.

Then they went downstairs and searched the cupboards for something to have for breakfast. Like the rest of their family in Hell Close they were sailing close to the wind financially. Indeed, they were dangerously near to being shipwrecked on the cruel rock of state benefits. Charles had filled in two sets of claim forms. Both times they had been returned with a covering letter explaining that they had been 'incorrectly completed'.

When the second form had arrived back, Diana had said: 'But I thought you were good at sums and English and stuff like that.'

Charles had thrown the letter across the kitchen and shouted, 'But they're not written in bloody English, are they? They're in officialese, and the sums are *impossible*.'

He sat down at the kitchen table to try again, but the computations were beyond him. What he did work out was that they could not claim Housing Benefit until their Income Support was known; and they could not claim Income Support until their Housing Benefit was assessed. And then there was Family Credit, which they were yet to benefit from, but which seemed to be included in the total sum. Charles was reminded of Alice in Wonderland as he struggled to make sense of it all. Like her, he was adrift in a surreal landscape. He received letters asking him to telephone but when he did nobody answered. He wrote letters but got no reply. There was nothing he could do but to return the third set of forms and wait for the state to give him the benefits it had promised. Meanwhile they lived precariously. They bartered and borrowed and owed fifty-three pounds, eighty-one pence to Victor Berryman, Food-U-R owner and philanthropist.

The milkman knocked at the door for his money. Diana looked around the kitchen and snatched a set of Wedgewood eggcups from the shelf. Charles followed her, carrying a silver apostle spoon. 'Ask him for a dozen eggs,' he said, pushing the spoon into her free hand.

Barry, the milkman, stood on the step keeping his eyes on his milk float. When the door opened he saw, with a sinking heart, that he was not going to be paid in cash, again.

Later that day, Charles was tying his broad bean canes together in the front garden, when Beverley Threadgold passed by, pushing her baby niece in an old high sprung perambulator. She was wearing a black PVC mini skirt, white high heels and a red blouson jacket. Her legs were blue with cold. Charles felt his stomach churn. He lost control of the canes and they fell to the ground with a clatter.

'Want some help?' asked Beverley.

Charles nodded, and Beverley came into the garden and helped him to gather the canes together. When Charles had arranged them wigwam fashion, Beverley held them together at the top and waited until Charles had tied them secure with green twine. She smells of cheap scent and cigarettes, thought Charles. I should find her repugnant. He cast around for something to say, anything would do. He must delay the moment of parting.

'When are we next in court?' he asked, though he knew perfectly well when it was.

'Nex' week,' said Beverley. 'I'm dreadin' it.'

He noticed that four of her back teeth were missing. He wanted to kiss her mouth. The sun came out and her split ends sparkled; he wanted to stroke her hair. She lit a cigarette and he, a vociferous anti-smoker, wanted to inhale her breath. It was madness, but he suspected that he had fallen in love with Beverley Threadgold. Either that or he was suffering from a virus that was affecting his brain – or at least his judgement. She was not only a commoner, she was common. As she started to move off Charles tried another delaying tactic. 'What an absolutely splendid-looking baby!' he said.

But baby Leslie was not, in truth, an attractive child. She lay on her back and sucked angrily on a large pink dummy and the pale blue eyes that stared up at the sky over Hell Close seemed old, like those of an old man disappointed by life. A rancid smell emanated from her. Her tiny clothes were not entirely clean. Beverley adjusted a fluorescent pink cellular blanket around Leslie's shoulders and took her foot off the brake of the pram.

Charles gabbled, 'Hasn't taken long to get to court, has it, our case?'

'Our' – what a precious word it was, signifying something shared with Beverley Threadgold!

'It's 'cos it's *you*,' said Beverley. 'They want you out of the way, don't they?'

'Do they?' said Charles.

'Yeah,' said Beverley. 'In the nick, where you can't do no harm.'

'Oh, but I won't go to *prison*,' said Charles. And he

laughed at the absurdity of the notion. After all, he was innocent. And this was still Britain, not some lawless banana republic ruled by a despot in sunglasses.

'They don't want you goin' round trying to get your mum back on the throne.'

'But it's the *last* thing I'd do,' protested Charles. 'I've never been so happy. I am, at this moment, Beverley, deliriously happy.'

Beverley dragged heavily on the last millimetre of her cigarette and then threw the burning filter into the gutter, where it joined many others. She looked at Charles's grey flannels and blazer and said: 'Warren Deacon's sellin' shell suits for ten pounds a throw, you ought to get one for your gardening. He's got some trainers an' all.'

Charles hung on to her every word. If Beverley advised it then he would find Warren Deacon, hunt him down and demand a shell suit – whatever it was. The baby started to cry and Beverley said, 'Ta-ra then,' and carried on down the Close. Charles noticed the blue veins behind her knees, he wanted to lick them. He was in love with Beverley Threadgold! He wanted to weep and to sing, to laugh and to shout. He watched her as she went through the barrier, he saw her spit with contemptuous accuracy at Chief Inspector Holyland's feet. What a woman!

Diana knocked on the window and mimed drinking out of a cup. Charles pretended not to know what she meant, forcing her to come to the front door and ask, 'Tea, darling?'

Charles said irritably, 'No, I'm sick of bloody tea. It's coming out of my effing pores.'

Diana said nothing, but her lip trembled and her eyes filled with water. Why was he being so horrid to her? She had done her best to make their frightful little house comfortable. She had learnt to cook his horrible macrobiotic food. She coped with the boys. She was even prepared to accept his silly pigtail. She had no fun. She never went out. She couldn't afford batteries for her radio, consequently she had no idea what records were in the charts. There was absolutely nothing to dress up for. Sharon had butchered her hair. She needed a professional manicure and pedicure. If she wasn't careful she would end up looking like Beverley Threadgold and then Charles would go *right* off her.

'Are you building wigwams for the boys?' she asked, coming out and touching the bean canes. Charles gave her a look of such withering contempt that she went back inside. She had cleaned the house and washed and ironed; the boys were out somewhere, there was nothing else to do. The only thing she had to look forward to was Charles's trial. She went upstairs and looked inside her wardrobe. What would she wear? She sorted through her clothes and selected shoes and a bag and was instantly comforted. When she was a little girl she had loved dressing-up games. She closed the wardrobe door and made a mental note to save her serious black suit for the last day of the trial – after all, Charles *could* go to prison.

Diana re-opened the wardrobe door. What should she wear for prison visiting?

24 Mechanicals

Spiggy was lying on Anne's floor in a pool of water at midnight. Anne was mopping up around him. She was wearing green wellingtons, jeans and a lumberjack's shirt. Her thick, blonde hair had escaped from the clutch of a tortoiseshell clip and cascaded down her back. Both of them were wet and dishevelled.

Anne had turned on the washing machine, gone out to visit her grandmother and returned to find the kitchen tiles floating in three inches of water. Spiggy had been sent for.

Anne asked: 'What did I do wrong?'

'Your hose is come loose,' said Spiggy, making an effort to sound the 'h'. 'Tha's all it is, but you done good! Ain't many women 'oo can plumb a washer in.'

'Thanks,' said Anne, pleased with the compliment. 'I must get my own tool set,' she said.

'Ain't yer 'usband got one?' asked Spiggy.

'I separated from my husband two years ago,' said Anne.

'Did you?' said Spiggy.

Anne was astonished, surely everyone in the English-speaking world knew her business, didn't they? Anne squeezed the mop into a galvanised bucket and asked, 'Don't you read the newspapers, Spiggy?'

'No point,' said Spiggy. 'I can't read.'

Anne said, 'Do you watch television, or listen to the radio?'

'No,' said Spiggy. 'They do my 'ead in.'

How refreshing it was to talk to somebody who had no preconceptions about her! Spiggy tightened the hose, then together they screwed the back plate onto the washer and pushed it in place under the formica worktop.

'Right,' said Spiggy, 'Owt else you need fixin'?'

'No,' said Anne. 'Anyway, it's very late.' Spiggy didn't take the hint. He sat down at the small kitchen table.

'*I'm* separated from *my* wife,' he said, suddenly feeling sorry for himself. 'Perhaps we can· have a drink at the club one night, play a few games of pool?'

Spiggy put his arm on Anne's shoulder, but it was not a sexual move. It was the chummy gesture of one separated washing machine mechanic to another. Anne considered his proposition and Spiggy imagined making an entrance at the Working Men's Club with Princess Anne on his arm. That'd teach his mates to sneer about his size and shape. A lot of women liked small, fat men. Look at Bob Hoskins; he'd done all right.

Anne moved out from under Spiggy's dolphin-like arm and refilled his glass with Carlsberg. She glanced at herself in the mirror. Should she cut her hair? She'd had the same style for years. Wasn't it time for a change? Especially now, when she was at rock bottom: a single parent living in a council house, being wooed by a small, fat man at midnight.

'Yes, why not, Spiggs?' she said, surprising herself. 'I'll get a babysitter.' Spiggy could hardly believe his luck. He'd get a film for his camera and ask one of his mates to photograph him and Princess Anne chinking glasses together in celebration. He'd get the photo framed and give one to his mother. She'd be proud of him at last. He'd buy a new shirt; he had a tie somewhere. He wouldn't make the mistake he made with most women: lunging at their bra straps on the first date, playing them his dirty joke cassette in the car. He'd go easy with her. She was a lady.

Reluctantly, he got to his feet. He rearranged his overalls around his crotch. He had acquired a van. It stood at the kerb outside. An amateur sign-writer had written, 'L. A. SPIGGS, HIGH CLASS CARPET FITER' on the side. The previous owner was British Telecom, it stated in the log-book. This was the only legal document in his possession. He had no driving licence, insurance or road tax. He preferred to take his chance and, anyway, where was he going to get the money? I mean, after he'd forked out for the van? Legality was expensive and so was petrol.

'Right, I'm off,' Spiggy said. 'Gotta get my beauty sleep.'

Women liked you to make them laugh, he'd heard. Anne saw him to the door and shook his hand on the doorstep. She had to bend slightly to do so. But Spiggy felt ten feet tall as he slammed the door of his little yellow van and sped out of the Close with his exhaust pipe popping. Anne wondered if she should have told Spiggy that 'Fitter' was spelt with two t's.

The noise made by Spiggy's van woke Prince Philip and he began to whimper. The Queen cradled him in her arms. She would send for the doctor in the morning.

25 Lying Down on the Job

On Sunday morning, Doctor Potter, a young Australian with child-care problems, took Philip's hands in her own.

'Feeling crook, Mr Mountbatten? A bit low?'

The Queen hovered nervously at the end of the bed. She hoped Philip wouldn't be rude. He had been the cause of so many embarrassing incidents in the past.

'Of course I'm feeling bloody *low*. I'm lying down!' barked Philip, snatching his hands away.

'But you've been lying down for – what is it. . . ?'

The Queen answered, 'Weeks.' The doctor glanced at the titles of the books on the bedside table. *Prince Philip Speaks*, *The Wit of Prince Philip*, *More Wit of Prince Philip*, *Competition Carriage Driving*. She said, 'I didn't know you wrote books, Mr Mountbatten?'

'I used to do a lot of things before that bloody Barker ruined my life,' he replied.

Dr Potter examined Philip's eyes, throat, tongue and fingernails. She listened to his lungs and the beating of his heart. She made him sit on the side of the bed and tested his reflexes by tapping his knees with a shiny little hammer. She took his blood pressure. The Queen held her husband down whilst blood was removed from the vein inside the left elbow. The doctor used a spot of the blood to check his blood sugar level.

'Normal,' she said, throwing the test strip into the wastebin.

'So, may I ask if you have made a diagnosis yet, Doctor?' asked the Queen.

'Could be clinical depression,' said the doctor. 'Unless he's trying to swing a sickie. K'niver look at your pubes, Mr Mountbatten?' she asked, trying to undo the cords on his pyjama trousers.

Prince Philip shouted, 'Sod off!'

'K'ni ask you some questions, then?' she said.

'I can answer any questions you may have,' the Queen said.

'Nah, I need to know if his memory's crook. When were you born, Phil?' she asked cheerily.

'Born 10 June 1921 at Mon Repos, Corfu,' he replied mechanically, as though before a Court Martial.

The doctor laughed: 'Mon Repos? You're pulling my leg; that's Edna Everage's address, surely?'

'No,' said the Queen, tightening her lips. 'He's quite right. He was born in a house called Mon Repos.'

'Your ma's name, Phil?'

'Princess Anne of Battenburg.'

'Like the cake, eh? And your Pa?'

'Prince Andrew of Greece.'

'Brothers and sisters?'

'Sisters, four. Margarita, married to Gottfried, Prince Hohenlohe-Langenburg, Officer in German Army. Sophie, married Prince Christopher of Hesse, Luftwaffe pilot. . . .'

179

'That's enough sisters, darling,' said the Queen, cutting in. Too many skeletons were coming dancing out of the cupboard – enough to supply a Busby Berkeley musical.

'Well, he's compos mentis,' said the doctor, scribbling on her prescription pad. 'Try him on these tranx, eh? I'll come back this arvo, take some urine. Can't stop now, I've got a list longer than a roo's tail.'

When they got to the bottom of the stairs, the doctor said, 'Trine clean him up, will ya? He stinks worse than a diseased dingo's den.'

The Queen said she would do her best, but the last time she had tried, he had thrown the wet sponge across the room. The doctor laughed: 'Funny how things turn out. I did my Duke of Edinburgh's Award y'know. Got a gold. Last time I saw your husband was in Adelaide. He was wearing a sharp suit and half a ton of pancake make-up on his face.' Doctor Potter hurried across the road. She had another house call to make in Hell Close. Poverty was hard on the human body.

26 The Show Must Go On

Harris was in mourning. His leader, King, had died under the wheels of a lorry delivering Pot Noodles to the service bay at the back of Food-U-R. Harris had barked a warning, but it was too late.

Victor Berryman had covered King in a piece of sacking and laid him inside a Walkers crisp box. He had then gone to the house of King's nominal owner, Mandy Carter, and broken the news to her. Mandy, who rarely fed King and often denied him shelter in his own home, sobbed over her dog's body. Harris watched her cynically. Poor King, he thought, he didn't even have a *collar*. He had nothing, not even a food bowl, to call his own.

Mandy Carter had rung the Council on Victor Berryman's phone and they had called round with a grey van, slung King inside a sack, thrown the sack into the back of the van and driven off. The Pack had chased the van for a few hundred yards, but had eventually given up and gone to their homes.

Harris had waddled back to Hell Close and crawled under the hall table. He had refused a meal (a succulent oxtail), which had caused the Queen some concern, but not for long, he noticed. As usual, she was too busy with Philip to give her dog the attention he needed.

After a short sleep Harris barked to be let out and ran through the back gardens of Hell Close until he reached Charles's cultivated plot. Harris scattered the compost heap around and then ran up and down the neat seed drills so painstakingly planted by Charles only the day before. He rested for a while, then jumped up and pulled Diana's white jeans down from the line, chased a robin and ran off to find and sexually harass Kylie, who was playing hard to get. If King had taught him one thing, it was that you had to be tough to survive in Hell Close. And now that King was dead Harris intended to be Top Dog.

The King is dead. Long live the King! thought Harris.

On Monday morning by the second post an airmail letter arrived.

Stage Door
Theatre Royal
Dunfermline Bay
South Island
New Zealand

Dearest Mummy,

I could hardly believe my *ears* when I heard the election result. Is it *too* foul, living on a council estate?

I said to Craig, the director, 'I shall *have* to go home, Mummy needs support.' But Craig said, 'Eddy, think about it, what can you *do*?'

And I *did* think about it and, as usual, Craig was right. It would be terribly unprofessional to leave a show halfway through a tour, wouldn't it?

Sheep! is doing great business. Many bums on many seats. It *is* a good show. And they are *such* a brilliant cast, Mummy! Real troupers. The sheep costumes are horribly hot to wear, let alone sing and dance in, but I have never heard a *word* of complaint from anybody in the company.

New Zealand is a little dull and a trifle behind the times. I saw a wedding party coming out of church yesterday and the bridegroom was wearing *flares* and a kipper tie. It was a hoot!

Craig has been a little depressed, but then he is never at his best in the rain. He needs the sun on his body in order to feel *whole*.

It was frightfully funny yesterday, one of the leads – Jenny Love – lost her sheep mask during her big number before the first act finale, 'Lift the Wool from your Eyes'. She completely *corpsed* and could hardly bleat a word. Well, Craig and I were on the floor but the audience didn't seem to notice that Jenny's mask had fallen off. To tell the truth Jenny has got rather an *ovine* looking face.

We're leaving for Australia next week. Advance bookings are very good, I wish you could see *Sheep!*, Mummy. The tunes are lovely and the dancing is terrific. We did have a few problems with the author, Verity Lawson. She and Craig had a major artistic disagreement about the slaughtering scene. Verity wanted a dead sheep to be lowered on a hook from the back of the stage, and Craig wanted the Ram (played by Marcus Lavender of *The Bill*) to perform a dance of death. In the end Craig won, but not until Verity had called in the Writers' Union and made things generally unpleasant. Well, enough of this theatrical chit-chat, I'm sending you a *Sheep!* baseball cap, and also a programme. As you will see under 'Tour Manager' I've changed my name to Ed Windmount. Ever the peacemaker, eh?

Love from Ed.

P.S. I have had a strange letter from Grandma telling me to rejoice because Everest has been conquered!

27 The Queen and I

The Queen met the daft teenager in the street as she was about to open Violet Toby's gate. He was wearing a baseball cap with 'E' written on the front. The Queen thought that 'E' must stand for 'Enjoyment' or possibly 'Elton', the popular singer. She asked about Leslie, his baby half-sister.

'She screams all night,' he said, and the Queen noticed that he had black circles under his eyes. 'She's wicked,' he added.

The Queen thought it was a little harsh to call a baby wicked. 'Is that her dummy?' she said, pointing to the huge rubber dummy he was wearing on a ribbon around his neck.

'No, it's mine,' he said.

'But aren't you rather old for a dummy?' puzzled the Queen.

'No, it's the business,' said the daft teenager, and he took a nasal block from amongst the voluminous folds of his trousers and stuffed it up his nostrils, and then, to the Queen's surprise, smeared it over his face. 'Have you got sinus trouble?' asked the Queen. 'No,' said the daft one. 'It gives me a buzz.'

As he walked away sucking on his dummy, the Queen warned, 'The laces in your shoes are undone!'

The daft teenager shouted back: 'They ain't *shoes*;

they're trainers. An' *nobody* does the laces up no more, 'cept dorks!'

The Queen called for Violet Toby and the two women walked to the bus stop, talking about the latest crisis in Violet's family. It was a sad story, involving marital disharmony, adultery and fractured bones. When they got on the bus they each grumbled about the fare.

'Sixty cowin' pee,' said Violet.

Half an hour later they were in the huge covered market picking up vegetables and fruit from off the cobbled floor and putting them into their shopping bags.

'Right as rain when they've had a wash,' said Violet, examining some large pears which were only slightly puckered.

They were surrounded by shouting market traders who were dismantling their stalls. Expensive foreign-made vans waited at the kerb with their engines running. Traffic wardens prowled like big cats at feeding time. The poor were scavenging what they could before the Council cleaning squads arrived. The Queen bent down to retrieve brown speckled cooking apples that had collected around a drain cover and she thought, what am I *doing*? I could be in Calcutta. She picked the apples up and dropped them into her bag.

When Violet and the Queen got onto the bus they held out their sixty pences to the driver, but he said, 'It's a flat fare of fifteen pee now, regardless of journey.'

'Since when?' said Violet, incredulously.

'Since Mr Barker announced it an hour ago,' said the driver.

'Good for Mr Barker,' said the Queen, as she put the unexpected gift of forty-five pence back in her purse.

The driver said, 'So it's two fifteen pees, is it?'

'Yes,' said Violet, throwing thirty pence into the little black scoop next to the ticket machine. 'For the Queen and I.'

28 Stepping Out

On Monday evening the Queen sat downstairs in Anne's living room, talking to Spiggy about scrap metal. Anne was upstairs getting ready to go out to the Working Men's Club and her mother had come round to babysit. Spiggy was dressed in his best, a new white shirt, a tie with a horses' heads design and black crimplene trousers, held up with a wide leather belt with a lion's head buckle. His cowboy boots had been reheeled and resoled. Earlier he had presented Anne with a single red plastic rose in a cone-shaped cellophane wrapper. The rose stood now, veering to the right, in a Lalique glass vase on Anne's side table.

Spiggy had taken enormous trouble with his toilet. He had cleaned out the dirt under his fingernails with his penknife. He'd bought a new battery for his razor. He had gone to his mother's for a bath and had washed and conditioned his long, shoulder-length hair. He had gone into a chemist's and bought a bottle of aftershave, 'Young Turk', and had splashed it around his armpits and groin. He had selected his jewellery carefully, he didn't want to look *too* flashy. He settled on wearing one thick gold chain around his neck, his chrome identity bracelet on his left wrist and just the three rings. The chunky silver with the skull and crossbones, the ruby signet and the gold sovereign.

Anne had dressed carefully in a figure-concealing A-line dress and flat shoes. She didn't want to encourage Spiggy into thinking that their friendship was to become a sexual affair. Spiggy wasn't her type; she preferred dark, slim, delicate-looking men. Spiggy's rampant masculinity scared her a little. Anne needed to feel that she was in control.

The Queen saw them to the door and watched as they got into the van. She thought, if Philip knew about his only daughter's assignation, it would *kill* him. She switched on the television and watched the news. According to the BBC, the country was about to undergo an exciting rejuvenation. All manner of things were to be changed. There would be cheaper gas and electricity and cleaner rivers. Trident was to be cancelled. There would be a maximum of twenty children to a classroom. There would be more money for schoolbooks, more doctors trained. New engineering colleges could open. Social security would be doubled. Late or missing giros were apparently to be a thing of the past.

The Queen watched as film footage was shown of out-of-work building workers as they besieged recruitment centres for what the BBC's industrial correspondent said was to be 'the largest public housing construction and renovation programme attempted in the country'.

Damp, cold houses were to be mere memories. The BBC's medical correspondent confirmed that the economies due to the reduction of damp-related illnesses (bronchitis, pneumonia, some types of asthma) would save a fortune for the National Health Service.

Then the outside broadcast unit took over and Jack Barker was seen on the steps of Number Ten Downing Street, waving the document that foresaw all these miraculous changes. The close-up showed the title to be 'The People's Britain!' Multi-ethnic faces, smiling ecstatically, surrounded the royal blue lettering of the title on the pamphlet.

Another camera angle showed the gates at the bottom of Downing Street. Shot from below, the gates appeared to dwarf the pressing crowds standing behind. Jack stepped up to a microphone which was placed in front of Number Ten.

'This Government keeps its promises. We promised to build half a million new houses this year and we have already given jobs to a hundred thousand construction workers! Off the dole for the first time in years!'

The crowd yelled and whistled and stamped its feet.

'We promised to cut the price of public transport and we did.'

Once again the crowd went mad. Many of them had travelled in by train, tube and bus, leaving their cars at home.

Jack went on: 'We promised to abolish the monarchy and we did. Buckingham Palace has been swept clean of parasites!'

A cut-away shot showed the crowd behind the barrier cheering louder than ever. Hats were literally thrown into the air.

The Queen shifted uneasily in her chair, discomfited by the enthusiasm shown by her former subjects for this particular achievement.

When the cheers had died away, Jack continued with fervour: 'We promised you more open government and we will give you more open government. So let us now, together, remove the barrier that separates the Government from its people. Down with the barriers!'

And Jack left the microphone and in the growing darkness strode along Downing Street towards the crowd. 'Jerusalem' blared out from preset speakers and men and women emerged from a parked van wearing fire-proof overalls and welding hoods. The crowd drew back as the men and women lit their oxy-acetylene torches and proceeded to burn through the metal bars of the gates. Jack was handed a hood and welding equipment and began to burn through his own section. The outside broadcast continued even though darkness had fallen and the blue flame of the torches provided the only illumination in Downing Street.

The Queen watched the extended news programme with growing excitement. She also admired Jack's sense of drama and his obvious flair for public relations. If only *she* had been able to call on the skills of somebody like Jack in the Buckingham Palace Press Office!

When the gates were brought down in a dramatic synchronised gesture, the crowd trampled them underfoot and surged into Downing Street, sweeping Jack along with them, and surrounded the front door of Number Ten. Fireworks exploded overhead and the faces that turned toward the sky carried expressions of happiness and hope.

Like the citizens in the crowd and those watching at home, the Queen fervently hoped that Jack's expensive-sounding plans for Britain would come to fruition. There was a damp patch on her bedroom wall that was growing daily; her giro was never on time; and was it right that there should be thirty-nine pupils in William's class and never enough books to go round?

The studio discussion that followed the news centred on the Thatcher years. The Queen found it too depressing to watch, so she turned over and watched John Wayne defending the weak against the powerful in the American Midwest. She wondered if she should call at the Christmases next door, where Zara and Peter were playing on the latest Sega game, Desert Storm, but she decided to leave them. She liked to watch cowboy films alone, without interruption.

When Peter and Zara returned they found their grandmother asleep in her chair. They switched off the television, quietly closed the living room door and put themselves to bed.

29 Apple Pie

Chief Inspector Holyland was on duty when the American television crew turned up at the barrier at Hell Close. The crew consisted of a cameraperson called Randy Fox, a cropped-haired individual of indeterminate sex wearing blue jeans, Nike running shoes, white tee-shirt and black leather jacket. Randy wore no make-up, but breasts were discernible. The presenter was an excitable young woman in a pink suit called Mary Jane Wokulski. Her golden hair blew in the wind like a pennant. The sound man, Bruno O'Flynn, held his microphone on high over the Chief Inspector's head. He hated England and couldn't understand why anybody *stayed*. For Chrissake, *look* at the place and the *people*. They all looked terminally ill. The director stepped forward. It was company policy that, when working in England, he should wear a suit, shirt and tie. It would open doors, he was told.

He spoke to the Inspector: 'Hi there, we're from NTV and we'd like to interview the Queen of England. I understand we have to check in here first. My name is Tom Dix.'

Holyland glanced at the ID card hanging from Dix's navy pin- stripe. 'There is nobody called the Queen of England living in Hellebore Close.'

'Aw, c'mon, fella,' said Tom, smiling. 'We *know*

she's here.' Mary Jane was preparing herself for the camera, outlining her lips with a black pencil and brushing golden hairs from her shocking pink shoulders. Randy grumbled about the light, and hoisted the camera into the crook of her neck.

Chief Inspector Holyland continued, secure in the knowledge that he had a brand new act of Parliament behind him and a coachload of policemen parked round the corner in Larkspur Avenue: 'In accordance with the Former Royal Persons Act, section nine, paragraph five, photographing, interviewing and filming for the purpose of reproducing the said practices in the print or broadcasting media is forbidden.'

Randy snarled, 'Guy talks like he's got a hot dog up his ass.'

Tom smiled wider at Holyland. 'OK, no interview today, but how about filming outside of her house?'

'It's more than my job's worth,' said Holyland. 'Now if you wouldn't mind, you're causing an obstruction.'

Wilf Toby was trying to pass through the barrier. He was returning from a futile attempt to sell a stolen car battery. The battery was being transported in the skeleton of a child's pushchair. Wilf crouched over the handle, looking like a monstrous nanny. He hadn't slept well, he had dreamt about the Queen. They were disturbing, erotic dreams. He had woken several times and felt ashamed of himself. He would have liked to have dreamt about Diana, but for some reason it was always the Queen who shared his bed in dreamland.

He half expected Chief Inspector Holyland to arrest him for his nocturnal fumblings and he was anxious to get through the barrier and get home and put the battery in the shed.

Mary Jane approached Wilf. 'May I ask you your name, sir?' she gushed.

'Wilf Toby.'

'Wilf, what's it like having the Royals as neighbours?'

'Well, y'know, it's like, well, they're. . . .'

'Just like you and me?' offered Mary Jane.

'Well, I wun't exactly say jus' like you an' me,' said Wilf.

'Just ordinary folks?' supplied Mary Jane. But Wilf was standing with his mouth open, staring at the eye of the camera. Two amazing things were happening to him: he was talking to a beautiful American girl, who was hanging onto his every word, and he was being *filmed* doing it. He wished he'd shaved and worn his best trousers. Mary Jane frowned slightly, to show the viewers at home that she was about to embark on a number of serious political questions.

'Are you a Socialist, Wilf?' she asked.

Socialist? Wilf was alarmed. The word had become sort of mixed up with things Wilf didn't understand or hadn't experienced. Things like vegetarianism, treason and women's rights.

'No, no, I'm not a *Socialist*,' said Wilf. 'I vote Labour, normal like.'

'So you're not a Revolutionary?' insisted Mary Jane.

What was she asking now, thought Wilf. He broke into a sweat. Revolutionaries blew aeroplanes up, didn't they?

'No, I'm not a *Revolutionary*,' said Wilf. 'I've never even been to an *airport*, let alone been on a plane.'

Tom Dix groaned and hid his face in his hands.

'But you *are* a Republican, aren't you, Wilf?' said Mary Jane triumphantly.

'A publican?' puzzled Wilf. 'No, I don't run a pub. I'm unemployed.'

Bruno sniggered and switched his tape off. 'Guy's got the brains of a suckin' *mollusc*. You wanna carry on?' Tom Dix nodded.

Mary Jane forced another smile. 'Wilf, how is the Queen reacting to her new life?'

Wilf cleared his throat. A host of clichés rose to his lips. 'Well, she's not *over* the moon, but then she's not *under* the moon either, if you know what I mean. She's sort of just *on* the moon.'

Tom Dix shouted, 'Cut!' He turned furiously to Mary Jane. 'Can we get back to *earth*, please? Jeezus!'

Mary Jane said, 'C'n I help it if the guy's a little *slow*. We're in an *Of Mice and Men* situation here, Tom. This is Lenny I'm talking to. Tolstoy he ain't.'

Wilf stood by. Should he go or should he stay? To his great relief, he saw Violet bustling towards the barrier. He gratefully relinquished his place as interviewee and pushed his battery home. He had every confidence in his wife.

At a signal from Inspector Holyland the coach full of policemen drove slowly round the corner and approached the barrier. The policemen on board hurried to eat the crisps and swig down the Coca-Cola they had been issued with only minutes before. They looked eagerly out of the coach windows, hoping for action. What they saw was Mary Jane attempting to interview Violet Toby, Inspector Holyland trying to part the two women and a frustrated television crew fighting to record an interview.

The Superintendent in charge of them ordered them to put on their helmets and 'disembark from the coach in an orderly fashion'. They did so. Within a minute the Americans and Violet Toby were surrounded by a blue circle of polite English policemen. Inspector Holyland extracted Violet and ordered her to go home. Then the Americans were escorted to their vehicle and warned that the next time they violated the 'exclusion zone code' they would be arrested.

Tom Dix protested, 'Hey, I gotta better reception than this in *Moscow*. Me and Boris Yeltsin put back a flagon of Jim Beam together.'

Inspector Holyland said, 'Very nice for you, sir, I'm sure. Now if you wouldn't mind getting into your vehicle and leaving the area of the Flowers Estate. . . .'

As their Range Rover sped away from the barrier, Randy shouted, 'You *mothers*!' leaving a whole crowd of policemen scratching their heads.

'*Mother*?' What kind of an insult was that?

The Queen looked out of her upstairs window. Good, the noisy Americans had gone. Perhaps now she could get to the shops.

30 Confidences

Trish McPherson drove her gaudy little Citroën car past the barrier and into Hell Close. She had three clients to visit. She would have to hurry, there was a case conference at Social Services that afternoon: the Threadgolds were demanding Lisa Marie and Vernon back. They had heard that both children had fractured various bones during their fostering by kindly Mr and Mrs Duncan.

Trish dreaded the Threadgolds' conferences. There were always tears and dramatic protestations of innocence from Beverley and Tony. Trish wanted to believe that they had never harmed their children but they would hardly admit it, would they? And Tony had a criminal record for violence, didn't he? There it was on the files: Grievous Bodily Harm on a sixteen-year-old burglar; criminal assault on a night-club bouncer; using abusive language to a policeman.

And then there was Beverley. She behaved appallingly during the case conferences, shouting, screaming and once getting up and threatening Trish with a clenched fist. They were obviously an unstable couple. The children were certainly better off with Mr and Mrs Duncan, who had a sand-pit in the garden and a veritable *library* of Ladybird books.

Trish drew up outside the Queen's house. She

threw a tartan rug over her bulging briefcase which lay on the back seat. She didn't like to remind her clients that she had other clients to deal with and a briefcase was so *official*-looking. It intimidated them; nobody who lived in Hell Close took a briefcase to work. In fact, hardly anyone who lived in Hell Close *went* to work. Trish liked to give the impression to each client that she just happened to be passing by and had dropped in for a chat.

The Queen watched out of the front window as Trish removed the stereo from the dashboard of the Citroën and placed it in her voluminous duffel-bag (made from a redundant camel blanket by the look of it, thought the Queen, who had visited Jaipur and been escorted by two hundred camels – the smell!). The Queen hoped that Trish would go elsewhere, but no, there she was, opening her gate. It was too tiresome.

Five minutes later, the Queen and Trish were sitting on either side of the unlit gas fire, sipping Earl Grey tea. Trish had supplied the tea-bags; they smelt faintly of camel, thought the Queen as she'd waited for the kettle to boil.

'Well, how *are* things?' Trish asked in a voice that invited confidences.

'Things are pretty frightful, actually,' said the Queen. 'I have no money; British Telecom is threatening me with disconnection; my mother thinks she is living in 1953; my husband is starving himself to death; my daughter has embarked on an affair with my carpet fitter; my son is due in court on Thursday; and my dog has fleas and is turning into a hooligan.'

Trish pulled her socks up and her leggings down. She was allergic to flea bites, but it was an occupational hazard. Fleas came with the job. Harris scratched in the corner and watched the two women lift the delicate tea cups to their lips.

Trish looked the Queen straight in the eye (it was important to maintain eye contact) and said, 'And I expect *you're* suffering from a lack of self-esteem, aren't you? I mean you've been right *up* there, haven't you?' Trish held one arm in the air. 'And now you're right down here.' Trish dropped her arm abruptly, as though it were the blade of a guillotine. 'You'll have to re-invent yourself, won't you? Find a new lifestyle.'

'I don't think there will be much *style* in my life,' said the Queen.

'Course there will be,' reassured Trish.

'I am too poor for style,' said the Queen, irritably.

Trish smiled her horrible understanding smile. She paused and dropped her head as if she were wondering whether or not to speak what was on her mind. Then, bringing her head up, as though being decisive, she said, 'Y' know, I happen to think that – and I mean this, though it's a hoary old cliché. . . .'

The Queen wanted to bring something heavy and solid crashing down on Trish's head. Black Rod's ceremonial stick would have served the purpose nicely, she thought. Trish reached out and took the Queen's rough hands in her own.

'. . . The best things in life *are* free. I lie in bed at night and look at the stars and think to myself, "Trish, those stars are stepping stones to the unknown." And I wake in the morning and hear the birds singing, and I say to my partner, "Hey, listen, nature's alarm clocks are right on time." Course, he pretends not to hear me.' Trish laughed, displaying her privatised teeth. The Queen sympathised with Trish's sleeping partner.

One of nature's alarm clocks defecated on the window. A long white streak like an exclamation mark trickled down the glass. The Queen watched its progress.

'So, how can I help you?' asked Trish, abruptly, now playing the practical, sensible Trish, the Woman Who Got Things Done.

'You can't help me,' said the Queen. 'Money is the only thing I need at the moment.'

'There must be something I can do,' insisted Trish.

'You could retrieve your briefcase,' said the Queen. 'A youth is running down the Close with it.' Trish flew out of the Queen's house, but when she got to the pavement there was no sign of the youth, or the briefcase. Trish burst into tears. The Queen smiled. She had told a black lie; it wasn't a youth who had stolen the briefcase. It was Tony Threadgold.

Later that night, Tony came round to see the Queen. He was holding a bulging file in his hand. When she had drawn the living room curtains and they were seated side by side on the sofa, he extracted a letter from the file and said, 'It's from a consultant at the 'ospital.'

The Queen took the letter from Tony and read it. In the opinion of the paediatrician, Lisa-Marie and Vernon Threadgold suffered from brittle bone disease.

'The envelope was still stuck down,' said Tony. 'Trish 'adn't even read it.'

The Queen understood at once that the diagnosis absolved Beverley and Tony from the charge of physically abusing their children. She heard banging and crashing coming from the upstairs of the Threadgolds' house next door.

'It's Bev,' said Tony, with a smile which lit up his face. 'She's cleanin' the kids' room.'

31 Eric Makes His Move

The next morning the Queen received an envelope addressed to:

> The Occupant
> 9 Hellebore Close
> Flowers Estate
> Middleton
> MI2 9WL

Inside was a handwritten letter written on blue note-paper.

To Her Majesty Elizabeth II, by the Grace of God of the United Kingdom of Great Britain and Northern Ireland, and of her other Realms and Territories Queen, Head of the Commonwealth, Defender of the Faith.

Erilob
39 Fox's Den Lane
Upper Hangton
nr Kettering
Northamptonshire

Dear Your Majesty,

Please allow me to humbly introduce myself. I am Eric Tremaine, a mere loyal subject, who has been horrified by what has happened to this country and its once great peoples. I know that that coward and traitor Jack Barker has forbidden your subjects to approach you like this, but I have decided to throw my towel into the ring and defy him. If it means that one day I will face execution for my presumption, then so be it. (I have already lost two fingers in an industrial accident, so I have got less to lose than most people.)

The Queen broke off reading, snatched the grill pan and threw two burning slices of toast out of the window. Black smoke filled the kitchen. She used Tremaine's letter to disperse it. When the room was reasonably clear, she carried on reading.

Your Majesty, I have put my head on the block and started a movement, it is called Bring Our Monarch Back, or B.O.M.B. for short. My wife Lobelia is quite good with words (see above for the amusing name of our house, evidence of Lobelia's handiwork!)

You are not alone, your Majesty! Many in Upper Hangton are behind you!

Lobelia and I are going into Kettering this afternoon to recruit members for B.O.M.B. Normally we keep away from the hurly-burly of big towns, but we have overcome our reluctance. The Cause is greater than our dislike of the metropolitan whirl that is Kettering in the nineties, I fear.

Lobelia, my wife of thirty-two years, has never been one to push herself forward. She had preferred in the past to leave more confident types such as myself to bathe in the limelight. (I am the Chairman of several societies, Model Railways, Upper Hangton Residents Committee, Keep Dogs in the Parks Campaign – there are more, but enough!)

But my retiring wife is prepared to approach total and absolute strangers and talk to them about B.O.M.B. in Kettering town centre, mark you! This is a mark of her disgust at what has happened to our beloved Royal Family. Jack Barker is pandering to the appetites of the people and trying to bring us all down to the level of the animals. He won't be content until we are all being sexually promiscuous in the fields and farmyards of our once green and pleasant land.

Pigs like Barker will not accept that some of us are born to rule and others need to be ruled, and ordered about for their own good.

Well, I must stop now. I have to call in at number thirty-one and pick up the B.O.M.B. leaflets. Mr Bond, the owner of the aforesaid thirty-one has kindly desk-top published the above-mentioned leaflets!

B.O.M.B. is yet small, but it will grow! Soon there will be branches of B.O.M.B. in every hamlet, village, town, city and urban conurbation in the land! Fear not! You will once again sit on the Throne.

 I remain, your Majesty,
  your most humble subject,
  Eric P. Tremaine

The Queen put Tremaine's letter on to Philip's tray.

She thought it might amuse him but when she returned twenty minutes later she saw that the breakfast had not been eaten and that the letter appeared to be unread: it was still tucked at the same angle under the bowl of cold porridge.

'I've had this rather amusing letter this morning, darling, shall I read it out to you?' she said brightly. The doctor had said that Prince Philip must be stimulated. 'It's from a chap called Eric P. Tremaine. I wonder if the "P" stands for Philip? Quite a coincidence if it did, eh?'

The Queen knew that she was talking to her husband as though he were a simple-minded slug, but she couldn't stop herself. He wouldn't talk, wouldn't move, wouldn't *eat* now. It was absolutely *infuriating*. It was time to call the doctor again. She couldn't watch him starve to death. He was so thin now that he didn't resemble himself at all. He had white hair and a white beard and, without his tinted contact lenses, his eyes looked like the colour of the stone-washed denim that people in Hell Close seemed so fond of wearing.

He suddenly lifted his head from the pillow and shouted, 'I want Hélène!'

'Who's Hélène, dear?' asked the Queen.

But Philip's head sank back. His eyes closed and he appeared to go to sleep. The Queen went downstairs and picked up the telephone receiver. It was dead. She jiggled the black knob about, but there was no reassuring purr in her ear. British Telecom had carried out their threat to cut her off because she hadn't paid her deposit.

She put her coat on and hurried out of the house,

clutching a ten pence coin and her address book. When she was inside the stinking telephone box she saw that it was flashing '999 only'. She felt like doing a little light vandalising, a bit of genteel telephone box smashing. Was Philip a 999 case? Was his life threatened? The Queen decided that it was. She rang 999. The operator answered at once.

'Hello, which service do you require?'

'Ambulance,' said the Queen.

'Putting you through,' said the operator.

The phone rang and rang and rang. Eventually a mechanical-sounding female voice said, 'This is a recorded message. All ambulance service lines are busy at the moment and we are operating a stacking system. Please be patient. Thank you.'

The Queen waited. A man stood outside. The Queen opened the door and said, 'Awfully sorry, it's 999 calls only.'

She had expected the man to show a certain displeasure but was not prepared for the panic she saw on the man's gaunt face. 'But I gotta ring the 'Ousing Benefit office 'fore ten, else I get left off the computer,' he explained.

The Queen looked at the watch she had worn since she was twenty-one. It was 9.43 am. Nothing was ever *simple* in Hell Close, she thought. Nothing ran to order. Everybody seemed to be in a constant state of *crisis*, including herself, she admitted.

The Queen looked around Hell Close. Telephone wires were connected to at least half of the houses, but she knew that the wires were only symbols of communication. Somebody somewhere, whose job it was to disconnect the impecunious, had pulled the plug and severed most of the Hell Close residents from the rest of the world. Telephone bills had a low priority when money was needed for food and shoes and school trips, so the kids weren't left out. She herself had raided the jar where she kept the phone bill money and bought washing powder, soap, tights, groceries and a birthday present for Zara. She had told herself that of course she would replace the money, but it had proved impossible on Philip's and her combined pension and Philip wasn't *eating*. How would they cope when he was cured of whatever it was that was ailing him and he regained his enormous appetite? The Queen was also waiting for back-dated Housing Benefit. She sympathised with the man.

'Come with me,' she said. Relations had been strained lately between her and Princess Margaret, but this was an emergency. As they crossed the road towards Number Four, the man told her that he was a skilled worker, a shop-fitter, but the work had dried up.

'Recession,' he said bitterly. "Oo's *opening* shops? I made "For Sale" signs for a bit, then I got laid off. 'Oo's *buying* shops?' The Queen nodded. On her rare visits to the town she had been surprised by the proliferation of 'For Sale' signs. Most of the shops on the Flowers Estate were ghosts, only Food-U-R seemed to thrive. The Queen remembered the day she had bought Harris Food-U-R's own-brand dog food for the first time. She'd had no choice, it was ten pence cheaper than his usual brand. Harris had refused it at first and gone on hunger strike, but after three days had capitulated, hungrily if not graciously.

They reached the front gate of Princess Margaret's house. The curtains were tightly drawn. Nothing of the interior of the house could be seen. The Queen opened the gate and beckoned the man to follow her.

'May I ask your name?' she said.

'George Beresford,' he said, and they shook hands on the front doorstep.

'And I'm Mrs Windsor,' said the Queen.

'Oh, I know 'oo *you* are. You've 'ad a bit of trouble yourself, 'aven't yer?'

The Queen said that she had and knocked on the door using a lion's head knocker. Movement was heard inside, the door opened and Beverley Threadgold, now working as Princess Margaret's cleaner, stood there, holding a drying-up cloth. She looked pleased to see the Queen.

'Is my sister there?' asked the Queen, stepping into the hall, pulling George with her.

'She's in the bath,' said Beverley. 'I'd offer you a cup of tea but I daren't; she counts the tea bags.' Beverley looked towards the ceiling, above which her new employer was wallowing in expensive lotions. She straightened her maid's cap and pulled a face. 'Look a right prat in this, don't I? Still it's a job.'

'Pay well?' asked George.

Beverley snorted. 'One pound, cowin' twenty pence an hour.'

The Queen was embarrassed. She decided to change the subject quickly.

'Mr Beresford and I would like to use the telephone,' she said. 'Do you think that would be possible?'

'I'll pay,' said George, showing the collection of warm silver coins he clutched in his hand. The Queen looked at the grandfather clock that loomed over them in the narrow hall. It was 9.59.

'You go first,' she said to George. Beverley opened the door to the living room. They were about to enter when Princess Margaret appeared at the top of the steep stairs.

'I'm awfully sorry,' she called down, 'but I must ask you to remove your shoes before you go into that room, the carpet shows every mark.' George Beresford blushed a dark red. He looked down at his training shoes. They were falling apart and he wasn't wearing socks. He couldn't possibly reveal his naked feet, not in front of these three women. His feet were ugly, he thought; he had hairy toes and split nails.

The Queen looked up at Princess Margaret, who was drying her hair with a towel and said, 'I'd rather not remove my shoes. Will the cord stretch into the hall, do you think?'

Beverley brought the phone to them, the cord unfurled and stretched to its full extent as it reached the threshold of the room. But George was able to dial.

He listened intently as it rang.

The Queen watched Beverley cleaning Margaret's windows and wondered how much the maids at Buckingham Palace had been paid. It was surely more than one pound twenty an hour.

Eventually George recognised the tone. 'Engaged,' he said. The grandfather clock struck ten. George panicked.

'I've missed my turn on the computer.'

'Try again,' urged the Queen. 'The computer's always breaking down, isn't it? At least that's what they're always telling me when I ring about my Housing Benefit.'

George tried again. No. Engaged.

George dialled a third time and on this occasion the phone was answered immediately. This threw him; he had never mastered the use of the telephone. He liked to look into the eyes of the person he was talking to. He shouted into the receiver,

"Ello, is this the Housing Benefit? Right, right. I was told to ring before ten but ... yes, I know, but ... it's George Beresford speakin'. I had this letter to ring before ten so I can get on the....' George stopped talking and listened. The sound of the hairdryer seeped down the stairs.

'Yes, but,' said George, 'the thing is,' he turned slightly away from the Queen and lowered his voice. 'See, I'm in a bit of trouble. I'm havin' to pay the rent out of my redundancy and the thing is ... it's gone....' He listened again. The Queen could tell from the way that he contorted his face that he was being told things he either didn't want to hear, had heard a dozen times before or didn't believe.

'Hang on!' George said into the phone, then, turning to the Queen he said, 'They say they've got none of my papers. They can't find nowt about it.'

The Queen took the phone and said, in her authoritative Queen's Speech tones, 'Hello, Mr George Beresford's advisor here. Unless Mr Beresford receives his Housing Benefit in tomorrow morning's post, I'm afraid I shall have to instigate a civil action against your Head of Department.'

Beverley giggled, but George didn't think it was funny at all. You couldn't afford to muck about with *them*. He was surprised at the Queen's behaviour, he really was. The Queen handed the receiver back and George heard the Housing Benefit clerk say that she would 'prioritise' George's claim. George put the phone down and asked the Queen what 'prioritise' meant.

'It means,' said the Queen, 'that they will miraculously find your claim, process it today and put your cheque in the post.' George sat on the stairs and listened while the Queen rang the doctor's surgery and asked if the Australian doctor could call again at Number Nine Hell Close to see Mr Mountbatten, whose condition had deteriorated.

The Queen and George Beresford said goodbye, put thirty-five pence on the hall table and left.

32 Shrinking

Dr Potter looked down at Philip and shook her head. 'I've seen plankton with more meat on 'em,' she said. 'When did he last eat?'

'He had a digestive biscuit three days ago,' said the Queen. 'Shouldn't he be in hospital?'

'Yeah,' said the doctor. 'He needs an intravenous drip, get some fluids in him.'

Prince Philip was unaware that the two women were looking at his emaciated body with such concern. He was somewhere else, driving a carriage around Windsor Great Park.

'I'll get a bag together for him, shall I?' said the Queen.

'Well, I gotta find him a bed first,' said the doctor. And she took out her personal phone and began to dial. As she waited for her call to be answered she told the Queen that three medical wards had been closed down last week, which had resulted in the loss of thirty-six beds.

'And we're losing a children's ward next week,' she added. 'God knows what'll happen if we get a few emergencies.'

The Queen sat on the bed and listened as hospital after hospital refused to admit her husband. Dr Potter argued, cajoled and eventually shouted, but to no avail.

There wasn't a spare bed to be had in the district.

'I'm gonna try the mental hospitals,' said Dr Potter. 'He's off his head, so it's kinda legit.' The Queen was horrified.

'But he needs emergency *medical* care, doesn't he?' she asked. But Doctor Potter was already talking. 'Grimstone Towers? Dr Potter, Flowers Estate Practice here. I've gotta bloke I wanna admit. Chronic depression, food refusal, needs intubation and intravenous fluids. You gotta bed? No? Medical Unit full? Right? Yeah? Tomorrow?' she asked the Queen.

The Queen nodded her head gratefully. She would do her best to get some nourishment down him tonight and then tomorrow he should be in the safe hands of the professionals. She wondered what Grimstone Towers was like. It sounded horrid, like the establishments one saw lit up by lightning in the opening moments of a British-made horror film.

33 Swanning About

Two hours before the trial was due to begin the coachload of policemen cleared the immediate area around the Crown Court. All the print journalists and radio and television reporters who had come to cover the case were taken to an ex-RAF camp just outside Market Harborough and spent the day locked inside a large room, where they were encouraged to consume the contents of too many bottles of British wine.

PC Ludlow was now in the witness box, trying desperately to remember the lies he had told during the previous hearing at the Magistrates' Court.

The QC for the prosecution, a fierce fat man called Alexander Roach, was leading Ludlow through his evidence.

'And,' he was saying, wobbling his jowls towards the dock, 'do you see the accused,' he pretended to refer to his notes, 'Charlie Teck, in this court?'

'Yes,' Ludlow said, also turning towards the dock. 'He's the one in the shell suit and pony tail.'

The Queen was furious with Charles, she had told, no *ordered* him, to have a short back and sides and wear his blazer and flannels, but he had stubbornly refused. He looked like, well, a *poor*, uneducated person.

Ludlow stumbled through his evidence without the benefit of his police notebook, the Queen noticed. Ian

Livingstone-Chalk, the barrister representing Charles rose to his feet. He smiled cruelly at Ludlow in the witness box.

Ian Livingstone-Chalk had been an only child. In youth his reflection in the mirror had been his closest companion. He was all style but no substance, being too concerned with the impression he thought he was making to listen properly to the clues given by his witnesses.

'Police Constable Ludlow, did you take contemporaneous notes on the day in question?'

'Yes sir,' said Ludlow quietly.

'Ah good,' said Livingstone-Chalk. 'Do you have the notebook in which you made these notes in your possession?'

'No sir,' said Ludlow, even more quietly.

'No!' barked Livingstone-Chalk. 'Pray, why not?'

'Because I dropped it into the canal, sir!'

Livingstone-Chalk turned to the jury, and once again smiled his carefully adopted cruel smile. 'You-dropped-it-into-the-canal,' he said, spacing out the words, inviting scepticism to fill the gaps. 'And pray, Constable Ludlow, do tell the jury what you were doing *at*, *on* or *in* the canal.'

Ludlow said in a whisper, 'I was rescuing a distressed swan, sir.'

Livingstone-Chalk looked blank.

Two jurors sighed, 'Ah' and looked at Ludlow with new eyes.

Charles said, 'Ridiculous!'

The judge ordered Charles to be quiet, saying: 'I'm surprised you should find the rescuing of a swan to be a ridiculous pastime, Teck, considering that until very recently your mother owned the entire British swan population. Proceed, Mr Livingstone-Chalk.'

The Queen glowered at Charles, willing him to be silent. Then she turned her eyes on Livingstone-Chalk and willed him to cross-question Ludlow about his fictitious swan-rescuing activities, but he ignored the heaven-sent opportunity and instead got bogged down in the minutiae of the fight. The jury got bored and stopped listening.

When Livingstone-Chalk eventually sat down, Alexander Roach QC leapt opportunistically to his feet. 'One last question,' he said to Ludlow. 'Did the distressed swan live?'

Ludlow knew he had to answer carefully. He took his time. 'Despite my best efforts at mouth to mouth resuscitation and heart massage, sir, I'm afraid the swan expired in my arms.'

The Queen laughed out loud, and the whole court turned to stare. When the Queen had regained control of herself, the case proceeded. Charles, Beverley and Violet gave their evidence in turn, each of their stories corroborating the others.

'It was a silly misunderstanding,' said Charles, when accused by Roach of inciting the Hell Close mob to kill PC Ludlow.

'It may have been a *misunderstanding* to you, Teck, but PC Ludlow here, a man who is capable of showing tenderness to a swan, was grievously harmed by you, was he not?'

'No,' said Charles, red in the face. 'He was not grievously harmed by me, or anybody else. Police

Constable Ludlow scratched his chin when he fell on the road.'

The whole court turned to look at PC Ludlow's bearded chin.

Roach said dramatically, 'A chin so scarred that PC Ludlow will need to wear a beard for the rest of his life.'

The clean shaven jurors nodded sympathetically.

As they left the court room at the luncheon recess, Margaret said, 'Where did Charles find Ian Livingstone-Chalk – chained to the railings outside the Law Society?'

Anne said, 'Charles is from Dorksville, USA, but even he could defend himself better than Livingstone-Chalk.'

Over bacon sandwiches in the court cafeteria, Diana asked the Queen, 'How do *you* think it's going for Charles?'

The Queen daintily removed a piece of gristle from her mouth, placed it on the side of her disposable plate and said, 'How did it go for Joan of Arc, after the taper was applied to the faggots?'

It was in his closing speech to the jury that Ian Livingstone-Chalk finally ruined any chances Charles might have had of being acquitted. He had turned to Charles's character and background, saying, 'And finally, members of the jury, consider the man before you. A man from a deprived background.' (A few jurors rolled their eyes here.) 'Yes, *deprived*. He saw little of his parents. His mother worked and often travelled abroad. And at a tender age he was sent away to endure the privations and humiliations of, first, an English prep school and then, the ultimate horror, a Scottish public school. The regime was cruel, the food inadequate, the dormitories unheated. Every night he wept into his pillow, longing for his home.'

(It was here the case was lost – one juror, an ironmonger, later to be elected Foreman of the Jury, whispered to another, 'Pass me a violin.') But Livingstone-Chalk continued, oblivious to the antagonistic atmosphere emanating from the judge and jury. 'Is it any wonder that this homesick boy turned to drink? Will any of us forget the shock when it was revealed that the heir to the throne was escorted out of a public house after consuming unknown quantities of cherry brandy?' (Charles was heard to mutter, 'I say, it was only one,' and was told to be quiet by the judge.)

Livingstone-Chalk continued, with the doomed flamboyance of a man executing a spectacular dive into an empty swimming pool, 'This pathetic, wretched man deserves our pity, our understanding, our justice. What he did *was* wrong, yes, it can *never* be right to shout, "Kill the pig," and to attack a policeman. No, most certainly not. . . .'

Charles muttered, 'But I *didn't*. Whose side are you on, Livingstone-Chalk?'

The judge ordered him to be quiet or face further charges for contempt of court.

Livingstone-Chalk wound up by saying, 'Show him mercy, members of the jury. Think of that little boy sobbing in the dorm for his mummy and daddy.'

There was not a wet eye in the court. One female juror stuck two fingers down her throat in an 'I want to vomit' gesture. As Livingstone-Chalk returned to his seat in the court, the Queen had to be restrained by Anne and Diana from leaping to her feet and squeezing on his adam's apple until he was dead. Beverley had taken Charles's hand and pressed it sympathetically, and Violet had said out of the corner of her mouth, 'They've got better briefs than him in Marks and Sparks, Charlie.'

Charles smiled politely at Violet's joke and was again rebuked by the judge, who said, 'The least you could do is to show some contrition, but no, you appear to find this case amusing. I doubt if the jury agrees with you.'

This monstrous leading-the-jury statement went unnoticed and unchecked by Ian Livingstone-Chalk, who was adding up his expenses in his bulging Filofax.

The Queen had showed no emotion when sentence was passed. Diana had burst into tears. Princess Anne had made an obscene gesture towards the jury and Princess Margaret had slipped a Nicorette tablet into her mouth. As Charles was led away to the cells below he mouthed something to Diana. She mouthed back, 'What?' but he had already disappeared.

Later, in the early evening the former Royal Family were gathered around the Queen Mother's bed, watching Philomena Toussaint spoon soup into the Queen Mother's mouth.

'Open you lips, woman,' grumbled Philomena. 'I h'ain't got all day y'know.'

The Queen Mother opened her lips and her eyes and drank the soup until Philomena scraped the bowl with the spoon and said, 'H'OK.'

The Queen said, 'I'm awfully grateful. I couldn't get her to eat a thing.'

Philomena wiped the Queen Mother's chin with the side of her hand and said, 'It's a shock to she, to learn she's grandchild has been sent to prison, with all the ragamuffins and riffraff.'

Diana was finding the heat oppressive in the small crowded bedroom. She went out and opened the front door. William and Harry were playing in the street with a gang of shaven-headed boys, who were rolling a tyre towards Violet Toby's bit of pavement. A small boy was hanging from inside the tyre.

Diana heard William shout, 'It's my cowin' turn nex'.' Her sons were now fluent in the local dialect. It was only their long hair that distinguished them from the other boys in the Close. And every day they beseeched her for a 'bullet-head' haircut.

Diana watched as Violet Toby propelled herself out of her front door, shouting, 'If that bleedin' tyre touches my bleedin' fence, I'll tan your bleedin' arses.'

Disaster was averted when the small boy fell out of the tyre and scraped his knees and palms on the road. Violet waved to Diana, yanked the screaming boy to his feet and took him inside her house to dab iodine on his wounds. Diana felt she ought to stop William, who was now climbing inside the tyre, but she had no strength for an argument, so she shouted, 'Bedtime at eight, Wills . . . Harry,' and went back inside the Queen Mother's bungalow.

As she adjusted her make-up in front of the small mirror over the kitchen sink, she tried once more to decipher the message that Charles had mouthed to her as he was being led away to prison. It had looked like, 'Water the Gro-Bags,' but he couldn't have been thinking about his stupid *garden* could he? Not at such a tragic moment.

Diana mouthed 'Water the Gro-Bags' in the mirror several times, then turned away in disappointment, for whatever else it *could* have been, it certainly wasn't, 'I love you, Diana,' or 'Be brave, my love,' or anything else that people said in films to their loved ones as they were taken from the dock to the cells below. She thought enviously of the scenes of jubilation when the jury had announced that they found Beverley Threadgold and Violet Toby not guilty of the charges brought against them. Tony Threadgold had run towards his wife and lifted her out of the dock. Wilf Toby had gone to Violet and kissed her, full on the mouth, put his arm around her thick waist and led her outside where she was cheered by other, less important, Toby relations, who'd been unable to get into the small public gallery. The Threadgold and Toby clans had gone off together in an excited group to celebrate in the Scales of Justice pub over the road.

The Royal Family had simply climbed into the back of Spiggy's van and been driven back to Hell Close.

34 All Together Boys

Lee Christmas was cleaning under his toenails with the clean end of a dead match when he heard the singing.

> God save our gracious King
> Long live our noble King
> God save the King.
> Da da da da
> Send him victorious. . . .

Lee got up from his bunk and peered sideways through the barred window of the cell door. His cellmate, Fat Oswald, turned the page of his book: Madhur Jaffrey's *Far Eastern Cookery*. He was on page 156, 'Fish poached in aromatic tamarind broth'. It was better than pornography any day, he thought, as he salivated over the list of ingredients.

Keys crashed at the lock and the cell door swung open. Gordon Fossdyke, the Governor of the prison, came into the cell accompanied by Mr Pike, the prison officer in charge of the landing, who bellowed, 'Stand for the Governor.'

Lee was already standing, but it took Fat Oswald some sweating moments to climb down from the bunk.

Gordon Fossdyke had once enjoyed a whole week

of fame when he had suggested, in a speech at a Conference of the Association of Prison Governors, that there was such a thing as good and evil. Criminals fell into the evil category, he claimed. During Fossdyke's glorious week, the Archbishop of Canterbury had given seventeen telephone interviews.

The Governor stepped up to Fat Oswald and poked his belly. Folds of flab looking like a porcine waterfall cascaded down his front.

'This man is grotesquely overweight. Why is that, Mr Pike?'

'Dunno, sir. He came in fat, sir.'

'Why are you so fat, Oswald?' demanded the Governor.

'I've always been a big lad, sir,' said Oswald. 'I was eleven pound, eight ounces at birth, sir.' Fat Oswald smiled proudly, but he received no smile in return.

Lee Christmas's heart was beating fast under his blue and white striped prison shirt. Were they intending to strip the cell? Would they find the poems hidden inside his pillowcase? He would top himself if they did. Mr Pike was not above reading aloud one of Lee's poems in the association period. Lee sweated, thinking of his most recent poem, 'Fluffy the Kitten'. People had been murdered for less.

The Governor said, 'You're having two new cell-mates. You'll be a little crowded, but you'll have to put up with that, won't you?' He paced the small cell. 'As you know, we show no favouritism in this prison. One of the prisoners is our erstwhile future King. The other is Carlton Moses, who will protect him from any undue harassment from his fellow prisoners. I have met our erstwhile future King and I found him to be a charming, civilised man. Learn from him, he has much to teach you.'

The door slammed shut and Lee and Fat Oswald were once again alone.

'Christ,' said Lee. 'Carlton Moses in our cell. 'E's seven feet tall, ain't 'e? What with 'im and you, there ain't gonna be room to bleedin' *breathe*.'

Ten minutes later, another double bunk was brought into the cell. Fat Oswald could hardly move in the narrow space between the two. Lee bragged to Fat Oswald about his short acquaintance with Charlie Teck. He was less enthusiastic about Carlton Moses, however. Rumour had it that Carlton had actually sold his grandmother, or rather, had exchanged her for a Ford Cabriolet XRI. Fat Oswald thought the rumour must be false. In his opinion it was hardly a fair swap. What use was someone else's *grandmother* to anybody?

Their speculation was cut short by the arrival of Charles and Carlton, who were holding sharp cornered piles of bedding in their arms.

It was the worst day of Charles's life. He hadn't expected to go to prison. But here he was. He'd been subjected to several gross humiliations since arriving: having his buttocks parted in the search for illegal drugs had possibly been the worst. The door slammed and the four men looked at each other.

Charles looked at Fat Oswald and thought, my God, that man is simply *grossly* fat.

Lee looked at Carlton and thought, he *did* swap his grandma for a car.

Fat Oswald looked at Charles and thought, I'll get him to talk about all them banquets he's been to.

Carlton looked at the cell and thought, this is *serious* overcrowding, man. I'm writing to the European Parliament 'bout this.

'How long you get, Charlie?' asked Lee.

'Six months.' Charles already felt he couldn't breathe in the cramped cell.

'Out in four then,' said Lee.

'If he behaves,' said Carlton, as he stowed his belongings on to the vacant top bunk.

Oswald turned his attention back to Madhur Jaffrey. He didn't know how to address royalty. Was it 'Sir' or 'Your Royal Highness'? He would get another book out of the prison library tomorrow, an etiquette book.

Charles stood on tiptoe and looked out of the little barred window. All he could see was a patch of reddish sky and the top branches of a tree which was covered in new lime green leaves. A sycamore, he said to himself. He thought about his garden waiting for him. The new shoots, sprouting seeds and pricked out plants would miss him. He feared that Diana would allow the compost to dry out in the seed trays and hanging baskets. Would she remember to remove the side shoots from his tomatoes as he had begged her to do? Would she give the Gro-bags a litre and a half a day? Would she continue to throw her vegetable peelings onto his compost heap? He must write to her immediately with full instructions.

'Do any of you chaps have some paper to spare?' he asked.

'Pepper?' Lee looked baffled.

'Writing paper,' explained Charles. 'Stationery.'

'You wanna write a letter?' asked Carlton.

'Yes,' said Charles, who had wondered if he had actually been speaking English or had slipped into the French or Welsh language unconsciously.

'You have to be *issued* with a letter,' explained Carlton. 'One a week.'

'Only *one*?' said Charles. 'But that's simply absurd. 'I've got masses of people to write to. I promised my mother. . . .'

But he became aware of a new, pressing problem. He needed to go to the lavatory. He touched the bell next to the cell door. His cellmates watched in silence as Charles waited for the door to be opened. Two minutes later Charles was jabbing at the bell frantically. His need was now urgent. One agonising minute later, the door was opened by Mr Pike. Charles forgot where he was.

'About time,' he said. 'I need to go to the lavatory; where is it?'

Pike's brow darkened under his peaked cap. 'About time?' he repeated, mocking Charles's accent. 'I'll tell you where the lavatory is, Teck. It's there.' He pointed to a container on the floor. 'You're in prison now, you piss in a pot.'

Charles appealed to his three cellmates, 'Would you step outside for a moment while I. . . ?' Their answer was unrestrained laughter. Mr Pike grabbed Charles's shoulder and led him to the pot. He knocked the plastic lid off with a shiny-booted foot and said, 'Urination and defecation takes place here, Teck.'

'But it's barbaric,' protested Charles.

'You're coming dangerously close to infringing the rules of this prison,' said Pike.

'What are the rules?' Charles asked anxiously.

'You'll find out what they are when you break them,' said Pike with great satisfaction.

'But that's Kafkaesque.'

'It might be,' said Pike, who had no idea what the word meant. 'But a rule is a rule and just because you used to be the heir to the throne, don't expect no favours from me.'

'But I wasn't, I. . . .'

Pike slammed the door shut and Charles, unable to contain himself any longer, hurried back to the plastic pot and added his own urine to that of Oswald and Lee.

Oswald said shyly, 'I've read a book by Kafka. *The Trial* it was called. This bloke is up for something, he don't know what. Anyway, he gets done. It were dead boring.'

To divert attention away from the thunderous sound of his own urination, Charles said, 'But didn't you find the atmosphere tremendously evocative?'

Fat Oswald repeated, 'No, it were dead boring.'

Charles adjusted his dress and once again went to the bell and pressed it, explaining to Lee, Carlton and Oswald that he had forgotten to ask Pike for a letter. But Pike had given instructions that the bell to Cell 17 was not to be answered. Eventually the sky darkened, the sycamore branch vanished and Charles removed his finger from the bell. He declined Lee's offer to lend him a book, saying, '*Fast Car* is not a book, Lee, it is a magazine.'

Carlton was writing to his wife and stopped frequently to ask Charles the spellings of the words:

'enough', 'lubrication', 'because', 'nipples', 'recreation', 'Tuesday' and 'parole'.

Oswald ate a whole packet of Nice biscuits himself, sliding each biscuit surreptitiously out of the packet without disturbing the wrapping or the other occupants of the cell.

When the overhead light went out, leaving only the red nightlight, the men prepared to sleep. Yet the prison was not quiet. Shouts and the sounds of metal on metal reverberated and somebody with a high tenor voice began to sing, 'God Bless The Prince of Wales'. Charles closed his eyes, thought of his garden, and slept.

35 Platinum

Sayako came out of the changing room in Sloane Street wearing this season's suit, as featured on the cover of English *Vogue*. Last season's suit lay on the changing room floor in an untidy heap. She surveyed herself in the full-length mirror. The manageress, svelte in black, stood behind her.

'That colour's very good on you,' she said, smiling professionally.

Sayako said, 'I take it and also I take it in strawberry and navy and primrose.'

The manageress inwardly rejoiced. She would now reach this week's sales target. Her job would be safe for at least another month. God bless the Japanese!

Sayako walked over on stockinged feet to a display of suede loafers. 'And these shoes to match all suits in size four,' she said. Her role model was the fibreglass mannequin which lolled convincingly against the shop counter, wearing the same cream suit that Sayako was wearing, the loafers that Sayako had just ordered and a bag that Sayako was about to order in navy, strawberry, cream and primrose. The mannequin's blonde nylon wig shone under the spotlights. Her blue eyes were half closed as though she were enraptured by her own caucasian beauty.

She is so beautiful, thought Sayako. She took the

wig from the mannequin's head and placed it on her own. It fitted perfectly. 'And I take this,' she said.

She then handed over a platinum card which bore the name of her father, the Emperor of Japan.

As the manageress tapped in the magic numbers from the card, Sayako tried on a soft green-coloured suede coat which was also being worn by a red-haired mannequin, who was doing the splits on the shop floor. The suede coat cost one penny less than a thousand pounds.

'What other colour do you have this in?' asked Sayako of the assistants, who were packing her suits, loafers, bags and wig.

'Just one other colour,' said an assistant (who thought, *Jeezus*, we'll have a drink after work tonight). She hurried to the back of the shop and quickly returned with a toffee-brown version of the sumptuous coat.

'Yes,' said Sayako. 'I take both and, of course, boots to match, size four.' She pointed to the boots worn by the red-haired mannequin.

The pile on the counter grew. Her bodyguard standing inside the shop door shifted impatiently. The limousine parked outside the shop had already attracted the attention of a traffic warden. He and the driver were glaring at each other, but both knew that the Diplomatic plates on the car precluded any possibility that a parking ticket would be attached to the windscreen.

When the Princess and her purchases had been driven away, the manageress and her assistants screamed and yelled and hugged each other for joy.

Sayako sat in the back of the limousine and looked at London and its people. How funny English people are, she thought, with their wobbly faces and big noses and their *skin*! She laughed behind her hand. So white and pink and red. What bodies they had! So tall. It wasn't necessary to have so much height, was it? Her father was a small man and he was an Emperor.

As the car set off on its journey towards Windsor, where she was staying at the newly opened Royal Castle Hotel, Sayako's eyes closed. Shopping was so tiring. She had started at 10.30 in Harrods' lingerie department and now it was 6.15 and she had only taken an hour off for lunch. And when she got home she had that puzzling book to read, *Three Men in a Boat*. She had promised her father she would read at least five pages a day. It would improve her English, he said, and help her to understand the English psyche.

She had already ploughed through *The Wind in the Willows*, *Alice in Wonderland* and most of *Jemima Puddleduck* but she had found these books very difficult, full of talking animals dressed in the clothes of human beings. The strangest of all had been *The House at Pooh Corner*, about a retarded bear who was befriended by a boy called Christopher Robin. Sayako had been told by her tutor in Colloquial English that the English had many words for shit. 'Pooh' was one of them.

At Hyde Park Corner the car stopped suddenly, the driver swore and Sayako opened her eyes. The bodyguard turned around to face her.

'A demonstration,' he said. 'Nothing to fear.'

She looked out of the window and saw a long

line of middle-aged people crossing the road in front of the car. Many of them were wearing beige anoraks that Sayako, a devoted shopper, identified as coming from Marks and Spencer. A few were carrying signs on sticks, on which the letters B.O.M.B. were written in red, white and blue.

Nobody appeared to take any notice of them, apart from a few impatient motorists.

36 Gift Horse

Spiggy rode into Hell Close on the bare back of a chestnut horse called Gilbert. When the horse drew alongside Anne's house, Spiggy cried: 'Ay oop!' and Gilbert stopped and began to eat the couch grass which grew alongside the kerb. Spiggy dismounted and led Gilbert down the path and up to Anne's front door.

'Wait 'til she sees *you*,' he told the horse. 'She'll be cowin' gobsmacked!'

When Anne opened the door and saw Gilbert's gentle brown eyes looking into her own, she thought she would melt into a pool on the doorstep. She reached her arms out and embraced the horse's neck.

'Where'd you get him?' she said brusquely.

'Bought 'im,' said Spiggy. 'From a bloke in the club. 'E's got nowhere to keep 'im.'

'And have *you* got somewhere to keep him?' asked Anne.

'No,' admitted Spiggy. 'I'd sunk a few pints and I just sort of took to 'im. He were tied up outside in the car park an' I just' sorta felt, like, sorry for 'im. He were only fifty quid, 'n' a roll of stair carpet. 'Is name's Gilbert! 'E's got new shoes on,' he said anxiously, wanting Anne to agree that Gilbert was a bargain.

Anne's practised eye told her that Gilbert was a fine horse.

'What's he been used for?' she said.

'Trekkin', the bloke said, in Derbyshire. But 'e's been on 'is 'olidays lately cos the trekkin' business went bust. 'E's got a lovely nature.'

Anne could see that for herself. Gilbert allowed her to run her hands along each fetlock and inspect the inside of his ears. He even bared his teeth when Anne looked into his mouth as though he were sitting in a dentist's chair and were cooperating with the dentist. Anne stroked his chestnut nose, then took his bridle and led him down the path at the side of the house and out into the overgrown back garden. There was no saddle, but she heaved herself onto Gilbert's back and they walked to the end of the garden and back again. Spiggy lit a cigarette and sat down on the wrought iron seat that Anne had brought from Gatcombe Park. He liked Anne, she called a spade a bleedin' spade. An' she wasn't a bad looker either – with her hair down, like it was now.

He had been proud of the sensation they had caused when they had entered the Flowers Estate Working Men's Club on their first date. He had been even prouder when Anne had beaten all his mates at pool. Gilbert was Spiggy's love token.

He reckoned her garden was big enough for Gilbert, providing he had a good gallop on the Recreation Ground once a day. Anne got off Gilbert reluctantly.

'I couldn't possibly afford to keep him, Spiggy,' she said. 'I can't afford to feed the kids properly.'

'I'll *keep* 'im,' said Spiggy. 'Tell me what he needs

an' I'll geddit.' While Anne hesitated he said, 'It's just that I ain't got one of the big gardens like you. We could sorta share 'im. Me dad were a gyppo, so I'm used to 'orses. I were ridin' 'fore I could tie me shoelaces. Go on Anne, 'elp me out. You've got room for a stable.'

Gilbert nuzzled Anne's neck. How could she refuse?

In the afternoon George Beresford came round to measure Gilbert for his stable. He returned later with Fitzroy Toussaint. They were carrying sheets of pink melamine that George had taken from a hair salon he had once helped to refurbish.

'It's not exactly stole,' he said to Anne, when she raised objections about the dubious history of the melamine. 'It's a perk of the job.'

Fitzroy agreed and told Anne he could get free computer paper for her and the kids. 'No problem,' he said, 'anytime.'

Anne drew a rough sketch of a stable, stipulated how high Gilbert's feed and water troughs ought to be, explained that Gilbert would need room to turn around and that the floor would need a drain and would have to be able to withstand copious amounts of horse urine. Fitzroy helped George to carry another load of melamine and then excused himself – it was time to go back to the office.

Mr Christmas watched over the fence. He was out on bail after his attempt to steal a ballcock from a DIY centre had been thwarted by an in-store security camera. He took a carrot from out of his trouser pocket and fed it to Gilbert.

'What you doin' with the 'oss shit?' he asked Anne.

Anne confessed that she hadn't given it much thought, though she conceded that, given time, it could be a problem.

'I'll take it off yer 'ands if you like,' said Mr Christmas, who had visions of selling it at a pound a bag.

'I don't propose to get it on my *hands*, Mr Christmas,' said Anne.

They were laughing when the Queen came into the back garden carrying a saddle, which she gave to her daughter.

The Queen was unable to imagine life without horses. Despite Jack Barker's warning it had been second nature to her to pack a saddle into the removal van.

'I brought this down from the boxroom this morning. It will need adjusting, but I think it will fit him,' she said, smiling at Gilbert and feeding him a polo mint.

''Ow's your lad gettin' on inside?' asked Mr Christmas of the Queen.

'I don't know, I've had no letter yet,' the Queen said as she fiddled with the saddlecloth and the saddle. 'I've written to him of course, and sent him a book.'

'A book,' scoffed Mr Christmas. ''E won't be allowed to have *that*.'

'Whyever not?' asked the Queen.

'Regulations,' explained Mr Christmas. 'You coulda stuck LSD microdots inside the pages or sprinkled cocaine inside that hard bit what keeps the pages together. . . .'

'The spine,' informed the Queen.

'One a my lads got 'dicted to drugs when 'e were in prison,' said Mr Christmas chattily. 'When 'e come out he 'ad to 'ave that cold chicken treatment.'

'Turkey,' corrected the Queen.

'Yeah, turkey! Din't cure 'im though. Says 'e don't care if 'e dies young. 'E says 'e 'ates the world and there's nowt for 'im to live for.'

'How very sad,' said the Queen.

''E were a miserable bugger when 'e were born. Din't smile till 'e were a year old,' Mr Christmas said dismissively. 'Din't matter how much I thrashed him, 'e still wun't smile.'

37 Dear Mummy

The following morning the Queen was cleaning out the drain in the front garden when the postman came up the path with a letter. The Queen pulled off her rubber gloves. She hoped the letter would be from Charles. It was.

Castle Prison
Friday, May 22

Dear Mummy,

As you see, I have enclosed a Visiting Order. I'd be awfully pleased if you would visit me. It is ghastly in here, the food is indescribably horrible. One suspects it is foul when it leaves the kitchens, but by the time it reaches us in the cells it is fouler: cold and congealed. Please, when you come, bring some muesli bars and fruit, something nutritious.

Please bring me some books. I am not allowed to use the prison library yet. And I am dependent on my cellmates, Lee Christmas, Fat Oswald and Carlton Moses's, tastes in reading material. They do not share my love of literature, indeed last night I had to explain to them what literature *was*, or rather *is*. Lee Christmas thought that literature was something you poured into a cat's tray. At present we are locked up for twenty-three hours a day. There are not enough prison officers to supervise educational or work programmes.

We take it in turns to exercise in the small area between the bunks. Everyone, that is, apart from Fat Oswald, who spends all day every day lying on his bunk reading cookery books and exuding noxious body gases. I accused him of being partly responsible for the diminution of the ozone layer, but he merely said, 'What's that when it's at home?'

Hell truly *is* other people, Mummy. I long to take a solitary walk, or spend the day fishing alone; just me, the river and the wildlife.

Is Diana working on my appeal? Do check, Mummy. It is monstrously unjust that I am here at all. I did *not* incite a riot that day in Hell Close. I did not shout 'Kill the pig'. Carlton said my brief, Ian Livingstone-Chalk, is well known for his laziness and incompetence. In criminal circles he is known as 'Chalk the Pork' because of his sympathy for the police. One wonders why he is a defence lawyer. Ask Diana to complain to the Bar Council about him, and *please* remind her to water the garden – the tomatoes in the Gro-bags by the kitchen door need at *least* a litre and a half per plant per day – more if the weather is especially hot.

The Governor, Mr Fossdyke, presented me with your portrait yesterday, the official Coronation one. I am sitting underneath it as I write. This has caused some resentment amongst my cellmates. They are demanding that Mr Fossdyke presents *them* with oil paintings of *their* mothers.

I wish that Mr Fossdyke would treat me with the contempt with which he treats the other prisoners. Please, could you write to him and ask him to look at me contemptuously the next time he sees me, speak to me harshly, etc. He would take notice of you; he's clearly an ardent royalist.

Do remember me to Wills and Harry and tell them that Papa is enjoying his holiday abroad. Give my love to Granny and my regards to Father.

As you can see, I made a mistake on the enclosed Visiting Order. I meant, of course, to put Diana's name after yours, *but* for some extraordinary reason wrote Beverley Threadgold's instead. I cannot think why. I hope Diana won't mind waiting a week or possibly two.

Love,
    your son Charles.

PS. The tomatoes need feeding with liquid manure once a week.

PPS Did you know that Harris had made a bitch called Kylie pregnant? Kylie's owner, Allan Gower, is in here, he is a 'plastic cowboy' (i.e. a credit card swindler). He is asking me for part payment of the vet's fees.

The Queen sat down and immediately wrote to the Governor.

Gordon Fossdyke Esq
The Governor
Castle Prison

9 Hell Close
Flowers Estate
Monday May 25 1992

Dear Mr Fossdyke,

As you know, my son is in your care. He writes to tell me of your many kindnesses. I am most grateful, but would appreciate it more if you were to be *unkind* to him occasionally. I wonder if you could arrange for him to be punished harshly for some minor infringement. I understand this might help to endear him to his fellow cellmates.

On another matter, why does the food served to prisoners have to be *cold*? Are you concerned about them burning their mouths, perhaps? I feel sure that there must be some reasons (of which I am unaware) because it is surely within your organisational skills to ensure that the food reaches the prisoners at what you and I would consider to be an appropriate temperature.

A small point. I sent my son a book, *Organic Gardening* by Alan Thelwell, over a week ago. Why has it not yet been given to him? An oversight perhaps?

Yours sincerely,
Elizabeth Windsor

The same morning Charles himself had received a letter.

Charles darling,

Sorry I haven't written before, but I've been so busy! I hope you are well!

I have had my hair tinted chestnut, everyone says it suits me. I found a *terribly* nice trouser suit in Help the Aged, it was Max Mara, sort of a blush pink/beige colour. With a longish jacket and tapered trousers. And only £2.45! I wore it to William's parents' evening with my white shirt (the one with the embroidered collar).

Last night I went to a dried flower party at Mandy Carter's. The idea is that you go round and buy some dried flowers and Mandy gets commission on what is sold. Your granny was there with her friend, Philomena. I bought a sweet little basket full of that blue stuff that smells so nice; there's a lot of it growing at Sandringham, but it's not heather. Oh you know what it's called, it begins with an 'L', I think. It's on the tip of my tongue. No, it's gone.

Not enough people bought things, so poor Mandy didn't make any money at all! The woman who demonstrated the dried flowers kindly offered to let me have a party next week, so I said I would! Money is very tight. Victor Berryman (Food-U-R) said it costs £400 a week to keep a prisoner in jail – Lucky you!

I must go now. I have just seen Harris jumping on the Gro-bags!!!

Love,
Diana.

PS. Lavender!
PPSSonny Christmas died in his sleep last night.
       Sad, isn't it! William got fourteen per cent in a
       maths exam. I told his form tutor that nobody
       is good at maths in our family, but he said,
       'You seemed to be able to work your income
       tax out all right'. What did he mean?

Charles re-read his wife's letter. He shuddered every
time he came to an exclamation mark. Each one was
a visible reminder of the differences between them.

38 Dancing Towards the Light

The Queen Mother's ailing body lay in her bed in her bungalow in Hell Close, but her spirit soared 36,000 feet above the clouds in a BOAC De Havilland Comet jet plane. Group Captain John Cunningham was at the controls. His reassuring voice informed her of the countries she was flying over on this non-stop flight: France, Switzerland, Italy and the northern tip of Corsica. It was 1952. They were travelling at the thrilling speed of 510 miles an hour. The picture changed. She was shooting rhinoceros with a big-game rifle; then she was beating out a frantic rhythm on the bongo drums, before strolling over to talk to General Charles de Gaulle and commiserate with him on the fall of France: then she was watching as the Duchess of Windsor's coffin was carried down the steps of St George's Chapel, Windsor; a moment later, she had changed into one of her gorgeous frocks and was sharing a box with Noël Coward. The show was *Cavalcade*. After the show they had supper at the Ivy.

Philomena Toussaint dipped a corner of a handkerchief into a glass of iced water and used it to moisten the Queen Mother's lips. It was 3.15 am. The Queen Mother felt the delicious coolness on her mouth and smiled her thanks, but she did not have enough strength to speak or to open her eyes. The

Queen had asked Philomena to call a doctor if there was a marked deterioration in her mother's condition during the night, but Philomena said, 'I hain't calling no doctor. She over ninety years old. She tired; she entitled to sleep forever in the arms of the Good Lord.'

Philomena brushed the Queen Mother's hair, applied pink lipstick to her mouth and rouge to her cheeks. She tied the blue ribbons of the Queen Mother's peignoir together and formed a pretty bow under her chin. Then she remade the bed and placed the Queen Mother's hands on top of the linen sheets. Philomena waited as the Queen Mother's breathing became shallower. The light in the room became brighter. A bird sang in the eaves of the bungalow.

When she judged it was time, she went into the living room next door, where the Queen was asleep, fully dressed, on the sofa. The Queen woke immediately, as soon as Philomena touched her shoulder. She hurried to her mother's bedside and Philomena put her coat on and went to break the sad news to the other relations that the Queen Mother was dying. The Queen held her mother's hand and willed her to stay alive. What would she do without her? Anne, Peter and Zara came into the room: 'Kiss her goodbye,' said the Queen. Diana arrived next, carrying Harry and holding William's hand. The boys were wearing their pyjamas. Diana bent down to kiss the Queen Mother's soft cheek and then encouraged the boys to do the same.

The tip tap of Margaret's high heels was heard outside in the street as she hurried behind Philomena. Susan, the Queen Mother's corgi, climbed onto the bed and lay on the bedspread, on the mound created by the Queen Mother's feet. Margaret embraced her mother passionately, then asked her sister, 'Have you sent for a doctor?' The Queen admitted that she had not, saying, 'Mummy is ninety-two. She has had a wonderful life.'

Philomena said, 'I axed her once if she would want pipes and t'ings put into she body and a machine to do she breathin' an' she say, "Heaven forbid".'

Margaret burst out, 'But we can't just sit here and watch her *die*, not in this ghastly little room, in this ghastly bungalow, in this ghastly close, on this ghastly estate.'

William said, 'She likes it here, and so do I.'

Word had spread in Hell Close and neighbours began to gather outside the front door. They spoke in quiet voices about their memories of the Queen Mother. Darren Christmas was made to dismount from his noisy moped and push it until he was safely out of earshot of Hell Close. And, as a mark of respect, nobody was allowed to steal from the milk float that morning.

Reverend Smallbone, the Republican vicar, called at the bungalow at eight o'clock, having been alerted by the newsagent, from whom he bought the only copy of the *Independent* to be found within a four mile radius. He stood at the Queen Mother's bedside and muttered inaudibly about heaven and hell and sin and love.

The Queen Mother opened her eyes and said, 'I didn't want to marry him, you know. He had to ask me three times, I was in love with somebody else!' And closed her eyes again.

Margaret said, 'She doesn't know what she's saying; she adored Daddy.'

The Queen Mother was Elizabeth Bowes-Lyon once more, seventeen, a famous beauty, swirling around the ballroom of Glamis Castle in the arms of her first love, whose name she couldn't quite remember. Thinking was becoming difficult. It seemed to be getting dark. She could hear voices in the distance, but they were growing fainter and fainter. Then there was darkness but in the far distance a pinprick of bright light. Suddenly she was moving toward the light and the light took her and encompassed her and she was no more than a memory.

39 Punctuation

It was Charles's turn to choose the station, so everyone in the cell was listening to Radio Four. Brian Redhead was talking to the ex-Governor of the Bank of England, who had resigned the day before. Nobody had yet been found to take his place. Mr Redhead queried, 'So, sir, you're telling me that, in your capacity as Governor of the Bank of England, even you, in your exalted position, did not know the terms of this Japanese loan? I find that hard to believe.'

'So do I,' said the ex-Governor, bitterly. 'Why do you think I resigned?'

'So how will the loan be repaid?' asked Mr Redhead.

'It won't,' said the Governor, 'the vaults are empty. In order to fund his lunatic schemes Mr Barker has successfully robbed the Bank of England.'

The cell door opened and Mr Pike held out letters, saying, 'Fat Oswald, from your mother. Moses, one from your wife, and one from your girlfriend.'

To Lee he said, 'Nothing, as usual.' To Charles he said, 'Teck, one, from a moron, judging by the writing on the envelope.'

Charles opened the envelope, inside were two letters.

Dear Dad,

I am alrite are you alrite

I now you are not on your holiday I seen Darrun Christmas an he tole me you was in the nick

Harris as wripped up all the plants in the gardin
Love Harry. 7 years.

Dear Dad,

Mum told us a lie that you was on holiday in Scottland. Are video has been stolen and also so has the candlesticks what belonged to that King George what reined years ago. Mr Christmas knows the bloke what took them. He said he is going to beat up this bloke and get are candlesticks back.

Are school is gettin a new roof soon. Jack Barker sent a letter to Misses Stricklan and she tole us in assembly yestardy.

Aunty Anne as got a horse called Gilbert. It lives in her back garden in a stabel. It is pink. The stabel not the horse. Will you send us some money from prison we have not got none.

Love from William.

P.S. Please write back soon.

Charles read the two letters with horror. It wasn't only his sons' abysmal use of the English language, the misspellings, the contempt shown for the rules of punctuation, the appalling handwriting. It was the contents of the letters. When he got out of prison he would *kill* Harris. And why hadn't Diana mentioned the burglary?

As he was folding the letter, the cell door swung open and Mr Pike said, 'Teck, your grandma's dead. Governor sends his sympathy and says you'll be let out for the funeral.'

The door closed again and Charles struggled with his feelings. His cellmates Lee, Carlton and Fat Oswald looked at him and were silent. Some minutes later Lee said, 'If I was let out I'd do a runner.'

Charles stared out of the cell window at the top branches of the sycamore tree and longed for freedom.

Later that morning, when Fat Oswald returned from his creative writing class, he handed Charles a piece of paper, saying, 'It's for you, to cheer you up.'

Charles raised himself from his bunk, took the paper from Oswald's pudgy hand and read:

> *Outside*
> Outside is cakes and tins of pop
> And you can go into a shop,
> To buy the chocolates that you like,
> Or training shoes: the best is Nike.

Charles realised that what he was reading was a poem.

> Outside is flowers and trees galore
> If we could leave the prison door.
> There is girls with pretty faces
> We could take them to nice places.

Outside is where we want to be,
Charlie, Carlton, Lee and me.

'I say, it's frightfully good, Oswald,' said Charles, who certainly agreed with the sentiments the poem expressed, though he abhorred the banality of the construction.

Fat Oswald heaved himself onto his top bunk, beaming with pride. 'Read it out loud, Charlie,' said Lee, who, until now, had not realised that he was sharing a cell with a fellow poet.

When Charles had read the poem aloud to his fellow cell mates, Carlton said, 'That's a *wicked* poem, man.'

Lee remained silent. He was burning with creative jealousy. In his opinion, his own 'Fluffy the Kitten' was by far the superior poem.

Charles lay on his bunk, the last line of the poem kept repeating itself in his head:

Outside is where we want to be,
Charlie, Carlton, Lee and me.

40 Women's Work

Philomena and Violet knew how to lay out a body. It was something they had learnt to do in the past when times had been hard. They hadn't expected to be needed in 1992, but their services were once again in demand. Few people in Hell Close could afford to pay for the services of an undertaker. Not unless they went into crippling debt or the cause of death was an industrial accident (in which case the employer was anxious to placate the family). Insurance policies were considered to be items of fabulous luxury, as exotic as having a holiday abroad or eating roast beef on Sunday.

Knowing how important it was to keep busy at such times, the women had sent the Queen out on various small errands. The Queen had gone willingly. Without her mother's lively presence, she found the bungalow horribly oppressive.

When the two women had finished their work, they went to the end of the bed and looked at the Queen Mother. She had a small smile on her lips, as though she were dreaming of something rather pleasant. They had dressed her in her favourite blue evening gown and matching sapphire jewellery twinkled on her ears and around her throat.

'She looks serene, don't she?' said Philomena, proudly.

Violet wiped her eyes and said, 'I never see the point of 'avin' the Royal Family, but she *were* a nice woman, spoilt but nice.'

They checked everything was tidy, then left the bedroom and began to clean the rest of the bungalow. They anticipated having many visitors over the next few days and they had sent Wilf to the shops for extra tea-bags, milk and sugar. Diana joined them in the kitchen. She had brought a bunch of purple flowers on long stalks. Behind her Ray-Bans, her eyes were swollen from crying.

'I picked these from the garden,' she said. 'They're for . . . the Queen Mother's lying in state, or whatever it's called.'

A pungent smell insinuated itself around the kitchen.

'They're *chives*,' said Violet, sniffing at the bouquet. 'They're 'erbs,' she explained.

'Oh, are they?' said Diana, blushing and confused. 'Charles will be so *cross* with me.'

'Don't matter,' said Violet. 'Only they do pong.'

'Lilies is what's needed,' said Philomena, 'but the t'ings is one pound twenty-five *each*.'

'What's one pound twenty-five each?' asked Fitzroy Toussaint, entering the kitchen.

'Lilies, the kind that smells so sweet,' said his mother. 'The kind the Queen Mother liked.'

Fitzroy had never actually met Diana before. He took her face, figure, legs, hair, teeth and complexion in with a practised glance. He saw that the black suit was Caroline Charles and the suede shoes with the pointed toes were Emma Hope. What wouldn't he give to take this blushing lady out to the Starlight Club for a few Margueritas and a session on the dance floor? Diana looked over the chives at Fitzroy. He was so *tall* and beautiful – those high cheekbones. And his clothes were Paul Smith, his shoes were Gieves and Hawkes. He smelt so delicious. His voice was as smooth as syrup. His fingernails were clean. His teeth were perfect. She had heard he was kind to his mother.

Fitzroy said to Diana, 'I'm going to buy some lilies, fancy a drive?'

Diana said, 'Yes,' and they left the oldies in the kitchen and headed for the florist's.

Diana walked around the front of the car towards the passenger seat but Fitzroy said, 'Hey! Catch!' and threw the car keys to her. Diana caught them, crossed to the other side of the car, opened the driver's door and slipped behind the steering wheel.

At the barrier, Inspector Holyland stared at Diana and Fitzroy and said, 'Are you prison visiting today, Mrs Teck?' Diana lowered her eyes and shook her head. Every morning since Charles had been imprisoned she had waited for a Visiting Order but it hadn't yet arrived. The barrier lifted and Diana drove out of Hell Close and towards a world she was more familiar with: smart cars, handsome escorts and expensive flowers. She drove down Marigold Road and passed the Infants School where Harry was running in the playground. He had his coat over his head and was playing muggers – his favourite game. She skirted the Recreation Ground and saw Harris leading a large pack of unruly dogs through a tunnel on the children's play area.

Fitzroy slotted a cassette into the car stereo. Pavarotti's voice filled the car – 'Nessun Dorma'.

'I hope you don't mind?' he said.

'Oh *no*, he's my absolute fave, I saw him live in Hyde Park. Charles prefers Wagner.'

Fitzroy said sympathetically, 'Wagner's bad news.'

He leaned forward and pressed another button and the sun roof opened. Pavarotti's voice escaped and attracted the attention of the Queen, who was standing outside Food-U-R, receiving the condolences of Victor Berryman. The Queen looked up and saw Diana driving Fitzroy Toussaint, who was sitting in the front passenger seat waving his arms to the music.

What *now*? the Queen thought and she picked her carrier bags up and started to trudge back to Hell Close.

As Diana sped down the dual carriageway which led to the town, she and Fitzroy joined in with the final bars of 'Nessun Dorma', adding their own comparatively puny voices to the sweet bellow that was Pavarotti's. On the opposite side of the road, heading toward the Flowers Estate, was a horse and cart. Traffic was lined up behind it; furious motorists peered ahead, waiting for an opportunity to overtake.

'It's my sister-in-law and her bloke,' said Diana as she passed them.

'They look like a pair of gypsies,' said Fitzroy disparagingly. 'And what *did* that horse have on his *head*?'

Diana glanced into the rear view mirror. 'It's the hat that Anne wore at Ascot last year,' she said, adding drily, 'It looks better on the horse, though.'

She was pleased when Fitzroy laughed. It was a long time since she had made Charles laugh.

As they passed the prison, Diana said, 'Poor Charles.'

Fitzroy said, 'Yeah, you must be lonely without him, I expect?'

Their eyes met for a split second. But it was long enough for them both to know that Diana was not going to be *too* lonely. There would be compensations. Diana blossomed.

Meanwhile, in Charles's garden, the sun was beating down. And the water was evaporating from the Gro-Bags and the hanging baskets and the seed trays, leaving the compost as dry as the Nevada Desert.

41 Reading the News

Next afternoon, Violet Toby knocked on the Queen's back door and walked straight into the kitchen. She was holding that day's edition of the *Middleton Mercury*. Harris poked his head out from under the kitchen table and growled at Violet, but she kicked out at him with the sharp point of a high-heeled shoe and he retreated. Violet found the Queen in the living room ironing a silk blouse. The Queen was having difficulty with the collar.

'Wretched thing keeps puckering,' she said.

Violet took the iron from the Queen, and checked the variable control switch. 'You got it on linen,' she said. 'Tha's why.'

The Queen switched the iron off and invited Violet to sit down.

Violet said, 'I wondered if you've seen this. It's about your mam.'

She handed the Queen the open newspaper. On page seven, under a report that a white tee-shirt had been stolen from a washing line in the early hours of Sunday morning in Pigston Magna, was another small news item:

FORMER QUEEN MOTHER DIES

The former Queen Mother, who in 1967 opened the

Casualty Department at Middleton Royal Hospital, has died in Hellebore Close, the Flowers Estate. She was 92.

The Queen gave the newspaper back to Violet who said, 'Don't you want to cut it out?'

'No,' said the Queen. 'It's hardly worth keeping, is it?' Then she noticed that the front page headline screamed: 'LOAN CRISIS: JAPAN ISSUES ULTIMATUM.' She took the newspaper back from Violet and read that Jack Barker had been closeted in an eight-hour meeting with Treasury Officials, and the Japanese Finance Minister the previous day. No statement had been issued to the waiting media.

The *Middleton Mercury*'s financial correspondent, Marcus Moore, wrote that in his opinion, Britain faced its gravest crisis since the dark days of the War. He continued indignantly,

'No details about the precise collateral for the multi-billion yen loan have been made public. Mr Barker's commitment to open government must now be seen as a sham. Why oh why, are we being kept in the dark? What has Britain pledged to give Japan? The *Middleton Mercury* insists, "WE MUST BE TOLD".'

'Interesting, this Japanese loan thing,' said the Queen as she handed the paper back to Violet for the second time.

'Is it?' said Violet. 'I couldn't care less about politics myself. It don't affect my life, does it?'

'But I thought you supported Jack Barker, Violet,' said the Queen.

'Yeah, I do,' said Violet, 'But he'll be out on 'is arse soon, won't 'e?'

The Queen thought about the worsening financial crisis and agreed that Violet could be right. As she folded the ironing board away, and put it in the understairs cupboard, she wondered how she would feel about returning to Buckingham Palace. It would be awfully nice to have other, unseen hands to do her ironing for her of course, but the prospect of resuming her official duties made her shudder. She hoped that Jack would find a way out of his difficulties.

42 Working with Wood

The next day in Hell Close the Queen was watching as George Beresford knocked the last nail into the coffin.

'There,' he said. 'Fit for a Queen, eh?'

'A beautiful job,' said the Queen. 'How much do I owe you?'

George was offended. 'Nowt,' he said. 'It were only a few off-cuts and I already 'ad the nails.' He ran his hands over the coffin. Then he lifted the coffin lid away from where it leant against the garden fence and tried it for size.

'Lovely fit, though I shouldn't say so myself.'

'I must pay you for your *time*,' insisted the Queen, who hoped that George's time came cheap. The Social Services funeral grant was not extravagant.

George said, 'I'm master of my own time now. If I can't help a neighbour out, it's a poor do.'

The Queen ran her hands over the lid of the coffin. 'You're a craftsman, George,' she said.

'I were apprenticed to a cabinet maker. I worked for Barlows for fifteen years,' he said.

The name meant nothing to the Queen, but she could tell from the proud tone of George's voice that Barlows were a well-respected firm.

'Why did you leave Barlows?' she asked.

'I 'ad to look after the wife,' he said, his face clouding over.

'She was ill?' asked the Queen.

'She 'ad a stroke,' said George. 'She were only thirty-three, never stopped talking. Anyroad, one minute she were waving me off to work, the next time I see 'er, she's in hospital. Can't talk, can't move, can't smile. She could cry though,' George said sadly. 'Anyway,' he continued, still with his back to the Queen, 'there were no one else to look after her. Wash 'er and feed 'er and stuff, and there were the little 'uns, our Tony and John, so I gave my job up. Then, after she'd passed on, Barlows had gone bust and all I could get was shopfittin' work. I could do it with my eyes shut. Still it were work. I'm not happy if I'm not working. It's not just the money,' he said. He turned round to face the Queen, anxious to make his point. 'It's just the feeling of . . . it's somebody needin' you . . . I mean, what *are* you if you're not workin'? I 'ad some good mates at the shopfittin',' he said. 'I've lived on me own for three year and I'd be watchin' a good telly programme and I'd be on me own and I'd think, in the morning I'll tell me mates about this.' George laughed. 'Pathetic really, i'n't it?'

'Do you still see your mates?' asked the Queen.

'No, it don't work like that,' said George. 'I can't *arrange* to see 'em; they'd think I'd gone soft.' He started to put his tools away into slots sewn inside a canvas bag. There was a home for each tool. The Queen noticed that 'Barlows' was stamped in black ink inside the tool bag. She took a sweeping brush and started to sweep the curled wood shavings into a heap.

George took the brush from her, saying, 'You shun't be doin' that.'

The Queen grabbed the brush back and said, 'I'm perfectly capable of sweeping a few wood shavings. . . .'

'No,' said George, regaining control of the brush. 'You weren't brought up to do the dirty work.'

'Then perhaps I should have been,' said the Queen, as she yanked the brush out of George's hands again.

There was silence between them, each concentrated on their work. George polished the coffin and the Queen put the shavings into a black plastic bag. Then George said, 'I'm sorry about your mam.'

'Thank you,' said the Queen, and burst into tears for the first time since her mother's death. George put his cloth down and took the Queen in his arms, saying, 'There, there, let it all out. Go on, you 'ave a good cry.'

The Queen did have a good cry. George led her inside his neat home, showed her the sofa, ordered her to lie down, gave her a toilet roll to mop her tears and left her to her own misery. He knew that she would prefer it if he wasn't there to watch her abandon herself to her grief. After fifteen minutes, when her sobs had subsided a little, he carried a tray of tea into the living room. The Queen sat up and took the cup and saucer that he offered her.

'I'm so sorry,' she said.

'I'm not,' said George.

As they drank their tea, the Queen tried to work out exactly how many cups of tea she had drunk since she'd moved to Hell Close. It must be hundreds.

'Such a comfort, a cup of tea,' she said aloud to George.

'It's hot and cheap,' said George. 'A bit of a treat

when you've got nowt. An' it breaks the day up, don't it?'

The Queen emptied her cup and held it out to be refilled. She wanted to rest a while before tackling the other funeral arrangements.

Spiggy and Anne knocked on the back door and came through.

'Your mam's 'ad a good cry,' said George to Anne.

'Good,' said Anne, and she sat on the arm of the sofa and patted her mother on the shoulder. Spiggy stood behind the Queen and squeezed her right arm in a clumsy gesture of condolence.

Anne said, 'Spiggy and I have sorted out how to get Gran's coffin to the church.'

'You've found somebody with an estate car?' asked the Queen, who had already worked out that a hearse and two cars for the mourners was financially impossible.

'No,' said Anne. 'Gilbert can pull the coffin.'

'On what?'

'On Spiggy's dad's cart.'

'Only needs a lick of paint,' said Spiggy.

'I've got some tins out the back,' said George, warming to the idea.

The Queen said, 'But Anne darling, Mummy *can't* be buried from the back of a gypsy cart.'

Anne, who in her former life had been associated with Romany causes, bristled slightly at this slur. However, Spiggy, whose body coursed with Romany blood, took no offence. He said,

'I c'n see your mam's point of view, Anne. I mean, it ain't exactly a state funeral, is it?'

George said to the Queen, 'Your mam wouldn't mind. Whenever I saw 'er in a carriage she looked happy enough.'

The Queen was too sad and tired to raise any more objections, so preparations went ahead that afternoon for a Hell Close-style state funeral. Black and purple paint were considered to be suitable colours for the fresh paintwork on the cart and George, Spiggy and Anne began to rub off the old carnival colours and prepare the cart for its more sombre outing in two days' time.

43 Indoor Pursuits

It was the night of the annual dinner of the Outdoor Pursuits Association of Great Britain at the National (formerly Royal) Geographical Society. The banqueting hall was full of men and women with weatherbeaten faces and hearty appetites. Canoeists chatted to mountaineers. Orienteers swapped anecdotes with proprietors of sports equipment shops. Most of the guests looked uncomfortable in their formal evening wear, as if they couldn't wait to change back into their rugged outdoor clothes.

Jack Barker was the guest of honour. He sat at the top table, flanked by an official of the British Canoe Union and the Chairperson of the Caving Association of Great Britain. Jack was bored out of his brain. He hated the outdoors, but at this particular moment he would gladly have climbed Ben Nevis backwards and naked rather than endure yet another interminable story about being trapped in a flooded cave. He pushed his soup bowl away – the soup tasted fishy.

'What's the soup?' he asked the Master of Ceremonies, who stood behind him.

'Fish, Prime Minister,' answered the flunkey.

By the time Jack was halfway through his Coronation Chicken he had begun to sweat and the colour had gone from his face.

The British Canoe Union official bent towards Jack and asked with concern, 'Are you all right, sir?'

'I'm not sure,' answered Jack.

Eric Tremaine, who was attending the dinner in his role as a member of the Caravan and Camping Club of Great Britain, watched triumphantly from a more humbly placed table as Jack was led away by the Master of Ceremonies.

'Most undignified,' Eric remarked to his neighbour, a free-fall parachutist, as Jack vomited uncontrollably into the water jug that he clutched in his hands.

When the contents of Jack's soup bowl were analysed in the laboratories of St Thomas's Hospital, the liquid was found to contain elements of a common weedkiller and a tiny proportion of a liquidised slug pellet.

As no other guest at the dinner had suffered Jack's fate, the conclusion drawn by the doctors at the hospital and the police forensic experts was that an amateurish attempt had been made to poison the Prime Minister.

Eric Tremaine sat inside his caravan in a layby near East Croydon next morning. He re-read the headline for the third time: 'P.M. SURVIVES SLUG PELLET ASSAULT' and threw his paper down in disgust.

44 A Walk up Cowslip Hill

The Queen woke early on the morning of the funeral.
She lay awake thinking about her mother, then got
out of bed and looked out of the window. Hell Close
was flooded in sunshine. She noticed that Fitzroy
Toussaint's car was parked outside Diana's house.

The Queen searched through a tangled mass of
flesh-coloured tights and eventually found a pair that
were not too badly laddered. She dressed in a navy
blue wool dress and rummaged around in the bottom
of the wardrobe for her navy court shoes. She went
into the box room and looked through the boxes until
she found a suitable hat: navy with a white petersham
ribbon. She tried the hat on in front of the bathroom
mirror. How like my old self I look, she thought. Since
moving into Hell Close she had lived in comfortable
skirts and sweaters. She now felt stiff and over-formal
in her funeral outfit.

She went downstairs and fed Harris, who was
waiting outside the back kitchen door, then made
herself a strong mug of tea, which she took outside into
the back garden to drink. She noticed that Beverley
Threadgold's washing line was pegged out with children's clothes, which swayed in the slight breeze. She
could hear the scream of Beverley's twin-tub as it built
up to its spin cycle. Looking across to Anne's garden

she could see Gilbert munching on a bale of hay. Now, all around her, she could hear water running and doors slamming and voices calling to each other as the inhabitants of Hell Close left their beds and prepared for the early morning funeral.

The Queen went back into the house, brushed her hair, applied a little make-up, collected her handbag, gloves and hat, and left by the front door. She crossed the road and went into her mother's bungalow. The curtains were closed, as was the custom in Hell Close, signifying that a death had occurred. Philomena was in the kitchen, buttering a heap of sliced white bread. Fillings for the sandwiches: orange grated cheese, slices of pink spam, and a block of beige meat paste lay on greaseproof paper, waiting to be inserted into the bread and made into sandwiches for the after-funeral reception. Violet Toby came in carrying a tray full of little cakes covered in various garish shades of icing.

'How kind,' said the Queen.

Beverley Threadgold was next, with a large fruit cake which was only a little burnt around the sides. Soon the little formica table in the centre of the kitchen was laden with food.

Princess Margaret arrived, draped in a black veil and said, 'People are putting horrid bunches of cheap flowers on Mummy's lawn.'

The Queen went outside just as Mrs Christmas was laying a bunch of cornflowers onto the grass. A note attached said:

'With grate sympathy from Mr & Mrs Christmas and the boys.'

Other Hell Close residents milled around reading

the floral tributes. There was one from Inspector Holyland, a traditionally shaped wreath in red, white and blue carnations. On the florist's card he had written:

'God bless you, Ma'am, from Inspector Holyland and the lads at the barrier.'

But the largest and most beautiful display was being carried across the road by Fitzroy Toussaint. Two dozen fragrant lilies surrounded by a cloud of gypsophila. A florist's van pulled up and more flowers and wreaths were placed on the grass by eager Hell Close volunteers. Tony Threadgold had picked lilac from the scabby tree in his back garden.

At 8.30 precisely, Gilbert trotted up outside the Queen Mother's bungalow, pulling the cart which had been transformed into a thing of beauty. The purple and black paintwork sparkled, the wheels had touches of gold inside the rims and the initials 'Q.M.' had been stencilled in her favourite colour, periwinkle blue, all around the edges of the cart itself.

Gilbert's bridle had been cleaned and polished, and his coat gleamed. New shoes had been bought for him to mark the occasion and he stepped out proudly, lifting each foot as though he were used to taking a central role in royal ceremonies. A hush fell over the crowd of Hell Close residents as Anne and Spiggy got down from the cart and entered the bungalow. Gilbert bent his head and started to munch on Inspector Holyland's wreath before Wilf Toby took the reins and jerked Gilbert's head upright.

A police car containing Mr Pike, the prison officer, and Charles entered Hell Close with a police driver at the wheel. Charles was wearing a dark suit with a black tie and a pink shirt. His pony tail was tied at the back in its now customary red towelling band. On his right hand he was wearing a handcuff. Mr Pike wore his prison uniform and a handcuff on his left hand. Charles had thought, why couldn't Diana follow the simplest of instructions? I asked for a *white* shirt in my letter. The car stopped and Charles and Mr Pike, joined at the wrist, got out and went into the bungalow. The Queen was disappointed when she saw Charles. She had hoped that he would, by now, have had a regulation prison haircut. And why was he wearing a *pink* shirt of all things, was it a symbol of his growing anarchy?

The coffin bearers assembled in the Queen Mother's bedroom. Tony Threadgold, Spiggy, George Beresford, Mr Christmas, Wilf Toby and Prince Charles, temporarily released from Mr Pike. Spiggy was nervous. He was a good eight inches shorter than the other men; would his arms reach the coffin or would he be left looking ridiculous, with his hands grasping fresh air? George checked the screws on the coffin lid and, watched by the principal mourners, the men heaved the coffin onto their shoulders. Spiggy was forced to stretch, but to his great relief the tips of his fingers made contact with the wood. The coffin was manoeuvred carefully through the small rooms and out into the street.

The crowd watched in silence as the men went to the back of the cart and slid the coffin along until it was perfectly placed and secured by its own weight. The Queen asked that a small posy of sweet peas be placed on top of the coffin and then the other flowers and wreaths were passed up until the cart resembled a flower stall in a market. Anne jumped to the front of the cart and took the reins and Gilbert moved off at a suitably funereal pace. Philomena stood inside the closed front door of the bungalow, waiting. When she heard the crowd move away and the clip clop of Gilbert's hooves receding in the distance, she opened the curtains wide to let in the sunshine. She then flung the front door open to let out the spirit of the Queen Mother.

The horse and cart and the mourners passed through the barrier. Inspector Holyland saluted smartly and avoided eye contact with Charles. The procession was followed at a distance by the coachload of policemen, who were ready to repel representatives of the media, should any be foolhardy enough to challenge the ban on their presence. It was only half a mile to the church and the adjoining graveyard, but Diana wished she hadn't worn her highest black court shoes, though once again she was on public display, if only to the people outside their houses watching silently as the procession passed by.

Victor Berryman came out of Food-U-R accompanied by his check-out women and an adolescent youth, a shelf-filler, wearing a back-to-front baseball cap. As the cart trundled by, Victor snatched the cap from the youth's head and gave him a mini-lecture on showing respect for the dead. Mrs Berryman, marooned by agoraphobia, watched sadly from an upstairs window.

The last stage of the journey lay ahead. Cowslip Hill,

where the little church was situated. Gilbert strained within the shafts of the cart and adjusted himself to the incline. A gang of men and women were planting trees at the side of the road and they laid down their spades as the procession went by.

'Trees,' exclaimed the Queen.

'Marvellous, isn't it?' said Charles. 'I heard it on Radio Four. Jack Barker has ordered a massive tree planting operation. I hope they've prepared the planting holes properly,' he said, looking back anxiously.

Diana was stumbling now and Fitzroy Toussaint, dazzling in his dark suit, took her arm solicitously. This was a woman who needed support, he thought, and he was the man to give it to her, he added, to himself. Though he knew in his heart that this woman was strong enough to survive alone one day, when she'd recovered her self respect.

Anne said, 'Ay oop,' as she'd been taught by Spiggy and Gilbert came to a stop outside the churchyard. The crowd of mourners filed into the church and became a congregation and when they were all in place the coffin was brought in and placed at the altar. The Queen had chosen 'All Things Bright and Beautiful' for the first hymn and 'Amazing Grace' for the second. The Hell Close congregation sang along with gusto. They knew the words and enjoyed the singing. Sing-songs in the pub started easily and did not usually stop until brought to an end by the landlord. The Royal mourners sang in a more restrained fashion, apart from the Queen, who felt strangely invigorated, almost released. She heard Crawfie say, 'Sing up girrl, open your lungs!' and she did, startling

Margaret and Charles, who stood at either side of her.

At the end of the funeral service the vicar said, 'Before we move on to the churchyard I'd like you to join me in a prayer of thanksgiving.'

'Vicar's won the pools,' said Mr Christmas to his wife.

'Shurrup!' hissed Mrs Christmas. 'Show some bleedin' respect. You're in church.'

The vicar waited, then went on, 'Yesterday an attempt was made on the life of our beloved Prime Minister. Fortunately, thanks to God's intervention all ended well.'

Princess Margaret said *sotto voce*, 'Fortunately for whom?'

But the Queen shot her a death ray look which silenced her.

The vicar continued, though his patience was wearing thin, 'Almighty God, thank you for sparing the life of thy servant, Jack Barker. Our small community has already benefited from his wise leadership. Our school is to get a new roof, there are plans to renovate our run-down houses. . . .'

'I got me giro on time!' interrupted a man called Giro Johnson from the back of the church.

'And I got a job!' shouted George Beresford, flourishing a letter from the new Ministry of Emergency House Building.

Other people called out their experiences of Jack's munificence. Philomena Toussaint began speaking in tongues and Mr Pike, carried away by the emotional atmosphere, confided that his dream for Castle Prison was to see flushing lavatories installed in every cell. 'We shall overcome!' he shouted.

The vicar thought, really, this is turning into a revivalist meeting. He had disapproved of the charismatic church ever since his wife had told him, during a quarrel, that he lacked charisma. After Charles had sung out that he thought the tree-planting scheme was 'proof of Mr Barker's care for the environment', the vicar decided enough was enough and ordered the congregation to kneel and put their hands together in silent prayer.

The moment when the coffin was lowered into the open grave was hard to bear for the Queen and she held her hands out to her two eldest children before she threw a handful of earth onto the coffin. Margaret's face hidden behind her veil showed disapproval; the Queen was showing her emotions – it was bad form, like peeling a sticking plaster away and displaying a wound. Charles grieved. Anne clutched at him and the Queen turned to both of them and tried to comfort them. Margaret watched with increasing alarm as Royal protocol was breached by Hell Close residents who, one by one, went up to the Queen and hugged her. And what was Diana doing in the arms of Fitzroy Toussaint? Why was Anne bent down and crying on that little fat man's shoulder? Margaret shuddered and turned away and began to walk back down the hill.

The funeral reception went on until late in the afternoon. The Queen talked happily about memories she had of her mother and circulated among her guests with an unforced informality. Meanwhile, Philomena Toussaint sat next door in her kitchen, listening to the sounds of jollity next door. She couldn't stay in a house where alcohol was being served. She took a chair, stood on it and started to rearrange all the tins and packets and cartons in her high cupboard. All the empty tins, the empty packets, the empty cartons, which represented an old woman's pride and a pauper's pension.

At the same time as the funeral reception was breaking up, Prince Philip, fortified by liquid food, sat up in bed and assured a contract nurse new to the ward that he was indeed the Duke of Edinburgh. He was married to the Queen, father of the Prince of Wales, and user of the Royal yacht *Britannia*, which cost £30,000 a day to run.

'Sure you are,' the nurse said in her lilting accent, looking closely at the wide-eyed lunatic. 'Sure you are.' She turned from Philip's bedside towards the patient next to him, who said loudly, 'I am the new Messiah!'

'Sure you are,' she said. 'Sure you are.'

Prince Charles begged Mr Pike to be allowed to see his garden and Pike, mellowed by two tins of extra strength lager, relented, saying, 'One minute, while I have a pee.'

Pike went into the upstairs lavatory and Charles whispered to Diana, 'Quick, find my shell suit and trainers.'

Diana did as she was told, whilst Charles looked

in horror at the dehydrated devastation that had once been his garden. The lavatory flushed and they heard Pike go into the bathroom to wash his hands. Diana watched as her husband threw off his funeral clothes and changed into the shell suit and training shoes. When she realised the significance of his actions, she ran to get her purse. She took out a twenty pound note and said, 'Good luck, darling, I'm sorry it didn't work out.'

Charles was running as Mr Pike dried his hands upstairs and he had leapt over the back garden fence as Pike opened the bathroom cabinet for a snoop; and he was on his way to freedom and the North, as Pike, his curiosity satisfied, closed the cabinet and headed downstairs to take the prisoner under escort back to prison.

June

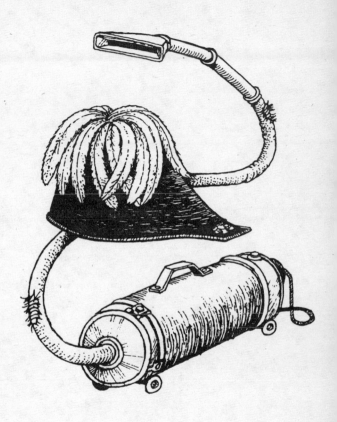

45 Near Miss

Jack Barker was entertaining a delegation from the Mothers' Union, who were petitioning for the legislation of licensed brothels. They were in the drawing room at Number Ten, eating little hot snacks and talking about flagellation and colonic irrigation. Jack was trying very hard to show that he wasn't at all shocked by the conversation of these respectable-looking middle-aged women.

'But,' said Jack to Mrs Butterworth the leader of the delegation. 'You wouldn't want a brothel next door to *you*, would you?'

Mrs Butterworth snatched a piece of crispy seaweed from a tray carried by a passing waitress and said, 'But I've *got* a brothel next door to me. The brothel keeper is a charming woman and the girls are as good as gold. Their garden is beautifully kept.'

Jack had a mental image of scantily dressed tarts whipping the borders into shape.

'So unfair,' said Mrs Butterworth, 'that they should live under the threat of prosecution.'

Jack nodded in agreement but his mind was on other matters. He was due to make a statement to Parliament in half an hour. He was dreading facing that angry bear pit and explaining how he was proposing to repay the Japanese loan. Rosetta

Higgins, Jack's personal private secretary, came into the room and signalled that it was time to leave. Jack shook Mrs Butterworth's hand, promised to 'address this most important matter', waved goodbye to the other women and left. Just before the door closed he heard Mrs Butterworth say to a cluster of women: '*Divine* eyes, nice bum, pity about the dandruff.'

As he came out of Number Ten, Jack brushed the shoulders of his dark jacket and thought, you fat old cow, I'll find out where you live and I'll have that knocking shop busted. He immediately regretted this vengeful thought. What was happening to him? He turned to Rosetta sitting next to him in the official car and said, 'Get me some Head and Shoulders later, will you?'

'Get your own,' she said. 'I'm working a sixteen-hour day as it is. When do *I* have time to shop?'

'Well I can't go into a shop, can I?' whined Jack.

The driver said, 'I'll get the bleedin' shampoo. There's a shop on the corner of Trafalgar Square. What kinda hair you got Jack? Greasy? Dry? Normal?'

Jack turned to Rosetta and asked, 'What kind of hair have I got?'

'Sparse,' she said.

Jack's hair clogged the drain of the shower in the mornings. As he rushed from meeting room to official engagement to Commons he left behind tangible reminders of himself. The hairs on his head detached themselves and floated away, looking for somewhere to settle. They no longer felt secure, or attached to Jack's head.

As the car left Downing Street and turned into

Whitehall, Rosetta handed Jack a file marked: 'B.O.M.B. UPDATE – CONFIDENTIAL'.

She said, 'You'd better see this.'

Jack smiled. Thank God for a bit of light relief. 'What's the old bugger up to now?' he asked.

Rosetta said, 'He's got the official support of the British Legion, the Caravan Club of Great Britain and the Federation of Allotment Holders, amongst others. Read it for yourself.'

Jack opened the file and began to read. Eric Tremaine was starting to be a bloody nuisance. His crackpot movement had spread out from Kettering and now encompassed most of the country. Marks and Spencer had completely run out of beige car coats with elasticated backs.

'Silly old sod,' said Jack, as he handed the file back to Rosetta. Then, 'Did the Queen ever write back?'

Rosetta snapped, 'Last page.' She threw the file into Jack's lap.

Jack opened it again, turned to the last page and read a photocopy of the Queen's letter which had been intercepted by the Post Office on its way to 'Erilob'.

9 Hell Close
Flowers Estate
Middleton
MI2 9WL

Dear Mr Tremaine,

Thank you for your letter. I am most grateful for the concern you and your wife express regarding my welfare and that of my family. However, I strongly advise you to concentrate on your many interests and hobbies, and forget about B.O.M.B. I would not want to be responsible for any difficulties you may find yourself in with the authorities.

I apologise for the crude stationery. The choice at my local shop is somewhat restricted.

Yours faithfully,
Elizabeth Windsor.

P.S. The contents of our correspondence will almost certainly come to the attention of the authorities. Therefore I must ask you to desist from writing to me again. I'm sure you understand.

The correspondence continued.

The driver stopped the car and hurried into the supermarket. Jack read a photocopy of another message from Tremaine which was written in his backward-slanting hand, on the back of an admission ticket to the Ideal Home Exhibition.

Your Majesty,
I understood your coded message: *'I'm sure you understand.'* That is why your milkman, Barry Laker, is hand-delivering this message, along with your pint of semi-skimmed. I will be in touch.

Yours,
Eric (B.O.M.B.)

The correspondence continued even further.

Your Majesty,

Forgive my silence. Lobelia and I had to go down to the caravan for a few days. Vandals had broken in and completely smashed one bunk bed and our shower fitting. Lobelia had to be sedated after seeing the damage, but she is now back in the saddle. B.O.M.B.'s membership increases by leaps and bounds. We have members as far afield as Dumfries and Totnes. Our postman (Alan) jokes that soon we will need our own pigeon-hole at postal headquarters!

Lobelia sends her affectionate regards to Diana (always her favourite). Mine are you and Anne, (for the good work she does with the dark kiddies abroad).

Yours affectionately,

Eric

It is safe to send a reply via your milkman, Barry Laker. HE IS ONE OF US.

The driver got back into the car and put a bottle of Head and Shoulders into the glove compartment.

There was still more in the Tremaine dossier. Jack sighed as he found himself reading the Queen's notes to the milkman.

THURSDAY
One extra pint please.
SATURDAY
One pot yog please.

MONDAY
May I pay you on Wednesday?
WEDNESDAY
Sorry Barry, giro didn't come.

Jack said, 'Is Barry Laker working for us?'

Rosetta said, 'No, he works for the dairy, he's a bona fide milkman who happens to be a member of B.O.M.B. Millions of people *are*, Jack. You should take them *seriously*.'

But Jack couldn't take B.O.M.B. seriously. As the car headed towards Parliament Square he removed the latest photograph of Eric and Lobelia Tremaine from the file and laughed out loud. The photograph had captured the pair in their front garden. Eric was pruning a Russian vine which had run amok amongst the upstairs guttering. His gormless face was turned towards Lobelia, who was caught by the camera as she handed Eric a digestive biscuit and a steaming mug. The time at the bottom of the photograph said '11 am'.

'Having his elevenses at eleven o'clock,' laughed Jack. 'Even though the stupid prat's up a ladder! And you ask me to take 'em seriously. And have you seen what that woman is *wearing*!' Jack pointed at Lobelia's photographic image.

Rosetta said, 'So, she's got no dress sense.'

Jack frowned at the Cenotaph as the car crawled past it. He said, 'It's not a question of dress sense, Rosetta. Her clothes are *mad*. They should be *certified*, locked away in an institution.'

Rosetta looked irritably out of the car window

at Whitehall. She didn't like Jack in this mood. She wanted a *serious* leader who didn't notice what people were wearing.

As the car approached the Houses of Parliament two police motorcycle outriders drew alongside. One policeman shouted, 'Drive straight past, follow us!'

The driver, recognising them as regular Commons duty police, did as he was told.

Rosetta said, 'Security alert.'

Jack said, 'Thank God for that.' His statement explaining Britain's parlous financial affairs with Japan would have to be postponed. As the car sped along Millbank, Jack looked at the Thames and thought how nice it would be to take a boat trip to Southend and then to the sea beyond.

In the early evening the Queen went into Patel's, the newsagents, to buy herself a bar of chocolate. When she was fabulously rich she hadn't cared for such things; but now that she was poor she craved confectionery. It was most odd. As she was gazing at the rows of brightly wrapped sweets she saw the late edition of the *Middleton Mercury* on the counter. A headline said: 'UPPER HANGTON MAN IN COMMONS PLOT SENSATION.' She read on, with Mr Patel's permission.

A local man, Eric Tremaine, was arrested in London earlier today and charged with possessing explosives. Tremaine (57) of Upper Hangton near Kettering was apprehended in the basement of the Houses of Parliament by a police dog and his handler. A shopping bag in the local man's possession was found to contain a small amount of Semtex. Tremaine, a retired fishmonger, was taken to Bow Street police station for questioning.

Best Kept Garden

Upper Hangton was still reeling from the shock when reporter Dick Wilson arrived to talk to residents. 'Eric was due to judge the Best Kept Garden competition on Saturday,' said Edna Lupton (85). 'I don't know what will happen now.'

Eccentric

A neighbour who did not wish to be named said: 'Eric was a bit of an eccentric, he never really got over losing the fish shop.' Mrs Lobelia Tremaine (59) is being cared for by friends. Eric Tremaine is the founder and leader of the Bring Our Monarch Back campaign (see page three for editorial comment).

The Queen turned to page three.

Today we report that a local man, Eric Tremaine, has been arrested in the possession of Semtex explosive by a plucky police dog and his handler. Your editor would like to congratulate the as yet unnamed dog. Who knows what dreadful calamity it averted? As readers know, this newspaper has supported Mr Tremaine in his campaign to restore the Monarchy and stop Mr Jack Barker's reckless spending of money he and the country do not possess. However, it would seem that Mr Tremaine's enthusiasm has led him to use violent means to gain his end. This newspaper does not, cannot, condone such tactics.

The Queen refolded the newspaper neatly and placed it back on the counter. She said, looking at Tremaine's smudgy front page photograph, 'He looks exactly as I imagined.'

'You know this man?' said Mr Patel.

'I was aware of his existence,' the Queen replied, as she hovered between choosing a Fry's peppermint cream bar and a tube of Smarties.

47 Poor Man at the Gate

The Queen sat in the day-room at Grimstone Towers. Philip sat next to her, wearing a white hospital dressing gown. Large green letters were stamped on the back, which read, PROPERTY OF NHS. Conversation had dried up between them. The Queen was reading *The Oldie* and Philip was watching the badly tuned television which was on a stand high on the wall. Other patients and their relations were chatting quite amicably. The Queen broke off from reading an article by Germaine Greer on the difficulties of gardening on a windy corner and glanced around the room. It was difficult to differentiate between patients and visitors, she thought. If only Philip would wear clothes again instead of nightwear. What was he mumbling about? She bent closer to her husband, the better to hear.

'Slant eyes,' he said, looking at the television.

The Queen followed his gaze and saw His Imperial Majesty the Emperor Akihito of Japan, waving from the top steps of an aeroplane. The camera angle changed and Princess Sayako was seen waiting at the bottom of the steps to greet her father. Jack Barker stood next to her, the sun glinted on his bald patch. Philip grew increasingly agitated.

'Slant eyes,' he shouted.

The Queen said, 'Hush dear!' but Philip got to his feet and went up to the television, waving his fists and swearing. The Queen now understood why the television had been placed so high on the wall. A male nurse led Philip away to his bed on the ward and the Queen followed. From the day-room came the sound of strange music, which the Queen instantly identified as the Japanese national anthem being played by what sounded like the band of the Coldstream Guards.

Later, when the Queen was walking down the drive of Grimstone Towers, towards the bus stop, she encountered a ragged group of unfortunates who had set up a temporary camp in the grounds. One of them approached her, a young man in a floor-length overcoat, and asked, 'Can we come back in, lady?'

The Queen explained that she was a visitor, not a hospital official.

'We want to come back inside,' said a middle-aged woman, with a child's voice.

A man with a battered face that the Queen found familiar shouted, 'We've been kicked out to live in the fookin' community. But we dinna like it and the fookin' community dinna like us. Yon Jack Barker shid let us in. He said he wid, so he did. He said he wid. And so he shid, so he shid.'

The Queen agreed with him and hurried to catch her bus.

47 Exit Stage Left

Barry the milkman knocked on the door of Nine Hellebore Close until his knuckles hurt. It was only 5.30 in the morning, but he had to make sure the Queen received the envelope *personally*. Lobelia Tremaine had insisted.

Barry heard Harris yapping upstairs and soon the Queen opened the door, bleary-eyed and with her hair unbrushed. Barry held the Queen's pint of semi-skimmed milk in front of him as though it were an orb. He glanced behind him at the barrier, then whispered, 'Message for you, your Majesty.'

The Queen took the milk from Barry and at the same time in one movement Barry passed the envelope.

'From Mrs Tremaine,' he said, quietly and turned away and went down the path.

The Queen sighed and closed the door. She had hoped that all that silly Tremaine business was over. She went into the kitchen and switched the kettle on. As she waited for it to boil she opened the envelope and read the enclosed pieces of paper. The first was hand-written on a notelet with a picture of a badger on the front. Inside it said:

Your Majesty,

As you may have heard, my husband Eric was arrested yesterday. This is a cruel blow to our Cause. However, I intend to take on Eric's mantle of responsibility, though I am only a frail woman. A well wisher from Australia has sent us the enclosed news item clipped from the *Sydney Trumpet.* . . .

The Queen did not finish reading the rest of Lobelia's note. She turned instead to the slithery fax.

POM PRINCE GOES WALKABOUT

Mystery disappearance of ex-royal tour manager

Ed Windmount, Tour Manager of *Sheep!*, currently packing them in at the Queen's Theatre, Sydney, vanished last night half an hour before curtain up. 'He left late this arvo to go to the theatre,' confirmed Clive Trelford, Manager of the Bridge View Hotel, 'and his bed has not been slept in.' Mr Craig Blane, the Director of *Sheep!*, said today, 'We are at our wits' end. Ed is usually so reliable. We fear the worst.'

A theatre electrician was the last person to see the ex-royal pom. The chief sparks, Bob Gunthorpe said, 'I was working over the stage and I looked down and saw a bloke built like a grizzly bear walking with Ed into the wings. I heard Ed shout, "Help!" but I didn't think nothing of it. Ed was a clumsy little runt, even for a pom, and I thought he'd tripped over a stage weight.'

Sydney police department have issued the following description of the man: 'Six-foot six tall, large build, tanned complexion, broken nose, diagonal scar running from left ear to mouth, wearing a green beret, camouflage jacket, green trousers and heavy boots'.

The Queen looked at the top of the fax, but there was no date. How long had Edward been missing? She had thought that at least he, the most sensitive of her children, had been spared unhappiness, but now, thanks to Lobelia bloody Tremaine, she had a new worry. She bent down and retrieved Lobelia's letter from Harris's jaws and completed her reading. At the bottom, after further drivel about B.O.M.B., she read the P.S.

P.S. I have it on good authority that Prince Andrew is serving in a submarine somewhere under the Polar Ice Cap.

'So *that's* why Andrew hasn't been in touch,' she said to Harris. 'Lucky Andrew.'

48 Out to Lunch

Anne and Spiggy had called round at midday to see the Queen and had been shocked to find her still in her dressing gown and slippers. Wordlessly she had given Anne the press cutting. Anne read it aloud, remembering courteously that Spiggy could not read. The Queen pushed her untidy hair out of her eyes and sighed deeply.

Anne said, 'I know it's yet another blow, Mum, but you can't let yourself go.' She led her mother to the stairs and ordered her to bath and dress.

'Spiggy's offered to buy us lunch,' shouted Anne later as the Queen dragged herself wearily out of the bathroom. The Queen thought, lunch? Where? A hot dog stand? A dual carriageway picnic? A wall outside a chip shop?

She was pleasantly surprised when Spiggy had signed them in to the Flowers Estate Working Men's Club (by making his mark). The lounge area was comfortably furnished and the Queen, who was ravenous, was pleased to see that a corner of the bar was piled high with meat, cheese and salad rolls, scotch eggs and slices of pork pie. There was even a murmuring television set in the corner which gave the room a nice homely touch. Through a gap in the door which led to the concert room the Queen could see pensioners like herself practising old-time dance steps to the recorded music of the Joe Loss band.

Violet and Wilf Toby were twirling together on the dance floor. Violet was wearing spangled backless high heels, a matching scarlet frock and a happy expression.

The Queen sank back onto the leatherette banquette seat next to Anne. She willed herself to relax.

Spiggy strolled up to the bar, taking out a roll of money as he went, and ordered their drinks and food.

As Norman, the lugubrious barman, assembled their order with his grubby hands, the Queen remembered Crawfie saying, 'You must eat everything put in front of you. It's awful bad manners not to!'

When the food and drink was in front of them Anne lifted her pint of bitter and said, 'Let's not talk about our family, eh?' to the Queen. A silence fell until Spiggy, after gulping down half a scotch egg, mentioned Gilbert. Then all three of them began an animated conversation about horses they had known and loved, which was only interrupted when Jack Barker's sombre face appeared on the television screen.

'Summat's up,' said Spiggy, after glancing at his watch. 'They usually 'ave kids' programmes on at this time.'

He shouted, 'Eh up, Norman, turn the sound up on the telly.' By the time that Norman had fumbled for the correct knob and adjusted the volume Jack Barker was saying, 'So, in view of the world financial crisis, which threatens this country's stability and indeed the very continuation of our way of life, your Government has decided that it will be necessary to make far-reaching constitutional changes.'

The Queen drained her glass of white wine and said sceptically, 'We have no written constitution. Barker is obviously going to write his own.' She leaned forward, eager to hear more of the proposals. But she was to be disappointed.

Jack Barker went on, 'Since I took office as Prime Minister it has been my privilege to introduce a radical programme of reform, despite opposition from many quarters. Whatever office I may hold in the future I will always endeavour to serve my people and my country.'

'Does that mean he's about to resign?' said the Queen.

'I 'ope not,' said Spiggy. 'It was only yesterday 'e abolished the cowin' poll tax!'

'Shush, Spiggs,' said Anne.

Jack finished abruptly, 'Tomorrow morning at eleven o'clock I will make a full statement to the nation. Good day!'

A presenter in a dark suit said in a sonorous voice, 'All programmes scheduled for tomorrow have been cancelled to make way for a special outside broadcast. These changes will affect all channels.'

'Christ!' said Norman, who, when he wasn't working, was a television addict. 'Must be the end of the cowin' *world*.'

49 Tea for Three

Jack hurried out of the Westminster television studio and was ushered into his car for the short return journey to Downing Street. Though the tyres of the car were rubber and the road beneath them was coated in tarmac, he fancied he could feel the iron rims of the tumbril beneath him as it went bumping over the cobbles.

In the bedroom of her *pied-à-terre* – a suite at the Savoy – Sayako stood in front of a looking glass. She was drinking in her reflection. It was perfect, perfect, as befitted someone who would soon be a world icon. Her servants had helped her off with the latest and most exquisite of many creations that had been specially designed for her and hung it, draped in tissue, inside a closet. Then Sayako, dressed elegantly but less gorgeously in one of her new Sloane Street suits, gathered up her bag and a copy of *Debrett's Peerage* and went downstairs to where a car was waiting to take her to tea.

When Jack's car drew up outside Number Ten he did not immediately get out, even though the driver had opened the door for him to emerge.

'Owt wrong, Jack?' asked the driver as Jack continued to sit. The word 'owt' resonated in Jack's head, again evoking the memories of his childhood and the principles he had formed then. His body stiffened. He looked like a dummy about to be used in a controlled collision for road safety purposes.

'Cramp,' lied Jack. 'Give me a minute.'

Inside Number Ten tea was being prepared on a low table by a pale-faced woman wearing silk. Jack's honoured guests waited in an ante room. When Jack eventually joined them he strode across the carpet shoeless and with his hand outstretched, only at the very last minute did he remember to drop his hand and bow instead.

50 Bird on the Wing

As the Queen was paying for her groceries at the Food-U-R checkout that afternoon Victor Berryman dropped something into her shopping bag. He whispered, 'Don't look now.'

When the Queen arrived home and unpacked her shopping she saw that the mystery object was a letter addressed to her in Charles's handwriting.

> The Wilderness,
> Far North

Mummy Darling,

A hurried note (I am constantly on the move) to tell you that I am 'over the sea to Skye' – not absolutely *literally* over the sea to *Skye*. But I am certainly in the *vicinity*.

I sleep during the day and move and forage for food at night. I try to be as one with the heather and, I think, succeed. It helps that my shell suit (blessed garment, *so* comfortable) is purple and green.

Before winter sets in I hope to find an abandoned croft and make it my home. My requirements are few: a peat fire, a bed of heather, simple food and perhaps a glimpse of the *Daily Telegraph* now and then.

One thing, Mummy, before I finish this letter. Please remember me to Beverley Threadgold, tell her that there was no time to say goodbye. And, of course, my regards to Diana and the boys.

A new life calls me. I need to feel the wind on my face and to hear the shriek of small animals as they are captured by winged predators.

Dearest Mummy, I send you my love,

C.

The Queen drummed her fingers on the kitchen table and said out loud, 'If I were a smoker I would certainly need a cigarette now.' She hated to think of Charles alone and on the run. How would the silly boy manage during the bleak Scottish winter when the very air froze? She opened a tube of Smarties, emptied it onto the kitchen table and picked out all the red ones.

51 Teeth

She had set her alarm clock for 7.15. Harris had not come home the night before. 'The wretch,' said the Queen. 'He knows I worry.' She set out to search Hell Close.

An hour later, the Queen switched the television on in the living room. The screen was filled with the front view of Buckingham Palace. The flagpole was bare. Martial music was playing – the Queen thought it sounded like the band of the Royal Marines. She dragged the vacuum cleaner free from its entanglement with the ironing board in the understairs cupboard. Though the picture hadn't changed since she switched it on, she still kept one eye on the screen as she vacuumed the carpet, cursing occasionally as the cleaner sucked up the loose strands at the edges that Spiggy had failed to attend to.

The Queen was anxious that the house should look its best. She had invited the family and some of the neighbours round to watch the outside broadcast with her. As she dusted and polished she noticed that her hands were trembling slightly and she realised that she had a terrible sense of foreboding about the nature of Jack Barker's announcement.

At 10.55 the small living room was crammed full of people. The Queen had to step over and around them as she served them coffee and biscuits. The television now showed the front door of Number Ten Downing Street and the crowds beyond, temporarily contained by a line of policemen with linked arms.

At exactly 11 o'clock the glossy black door of Number Ten opened and Jack Barker came out alone. He looked pale and tired, thought the Queen, as though he had been up all night. He walked over to the bank of microphones and held up his hand to quieten the cheering crowd. He looked down at his feet then lifted his head and said, 'My fellow Britons, last night I signed a document that will change all of our lives for the better. The other signatory was his Imperial Majesty, the Emperor Akihito of Japan.' Jack reached inside his jacket pocket and took out a piece of paper which he held in the air for the benefit of the television cameras and the hordes of newspaper photographers.

The Queen said, 'Get *on* with it, man!'

Jack eventually replaced the paper inside his jacket pocket and resumed speaking. 'As from today, England, Scotland, Wales and Northern Ireland have entered into a Treaty of Friendship with Japan, which will cement the special relationship and the ever-increasing ties, which already exist between our two great countries and bring us new security and prosperity.'

The Queen said, 'Cut the platitudes, Barker. Get down to it.'

Jack forced himself to look into the lens of the camera in front of him, as if, by maintaining eye contact with the millions watching, he could convince them of his sincerity. 'I am proud and happy to be able to tell you that this treaty will put Britain back on the road to greatness. Once more we shall be part of a worldwide empire on which the sun never sets.'

Most of the crowd cheered.

The Queen muttered, 'What's he up to?'

Jack went on, 'Since April the tenth I have served you as your Prime Minister. From today I shall continue to reside here at Number Ten Downing Street and to serve you in my new role as Governor General of Great Britain.'

The Queen shouted, '*Governor General*!' but the others in the room told her to be quiet.

Jack went on. 'We now share the sovereignty of this country with the Empire of Japan.'

The Queen could not restrain herself, 'He's sold us,' she shouted, 'as though we were a commodity!'

Jack continued, 'As a result of these constitutional changes, the temporary loan of 12,000 billion yen which my government negotiated on April the thirteenth, and which was due to be repaid by June the first, has been extended indefinitely. Our new federal relationship with the growing Japanese empire – which will be carefully balanced by a strong element of subsidiarity – will ensure that, at long last, we have the resources we need to rebuild our great country, as we want and deserve. It only remains for this political and financial alliance to be cemented further by a personal alliance. I am delighted to announce that this is happening, at this very moment!' The black door opened and Jack scuttled inside.

'What was all *that* about?' said Spiggy, baffled by

all the long words.

'Jack Barker has mortgaged this country to the Bank of Japan,' cried the Queen.

'Christ!' said Violet. 'Will we all have to talk Japanese?'

'Well I shan't,' said Wilf. 'I'm too old to learn a new cowin' language and anyroad I can 'ardly talk English.'

Beverley Threadgold said, 'I knew a bloke who went to a Japanese restaurant once. He said it was 'orrible. All 'e got to eat was raw fish.'

Violet said indignantly, 'Well, they needn't think they can come over 'ere thinkin' they can stop us cookin' our fish, 'cos I for one won't stand for it.'

Philomena Toussaint said, 'Who we pay our rent to? Is it still the Council or the Bank of Japan?'

Margaret drawled, 'If we had a proper written constitution, this couldn't happen.'

The Queen had to leave the room. She thought her head would explode. Was she the only one to realise the full significance of Barker's announcement? A coup had already taken place. Britain had been annexed and was now just another Japanese offshore island. She went into the back garden. There was still no sign of Harris. Yesterday's food was still in its bowl. The Queen threw it into the pedal bin under the sink.

She thought, it's a good job that Philip has gone mad. If he knew that his beloved adopted country had been sold like a fish in the market place it would send him, well, mad.

The Queen picked up her Sony portable radio and hurled it against the kitchen wall. Anne appeared in the doorway and said, 'Mum, come and see this.'

The television was now showing the Mall which was lined with crowds of people. Some were waving little union jacks but others were waving flags which depicted the rising sun. It was obvious to the Queen, who was an expert on such matters, that the crowds had no idea why they were there. They had gathered because crowd barriers had been erected.

Fitzroy was explaining to Diana that his job could be at stake. He was a recession accountant, he reminded her, and if there was no longer a recession where would that leave him?

The camera switched from the faces of the crowd to show a golden coach being pulled by four plumed white horses as it passed under Admiralty Arch and processed up The Mall. The crowd cheered automatically, even though the curtains inside the coach were drawn and it was impossible to see the occupants.

The Queen yelled, 'They would cheer for *chimpanzees*, the fools!'

Anne said, 'That's what *we* were, Mum. We lived in a bloody zoo to be gawped at by the public. I'm glad I'm out of it.'

The Queen noticed that Spiggy had inched slightly closer to Anne on the sofa. The room had become oppressively hot. She felt she would have to get some fresh air soon. Her temples throbbed.

As the coach turned into the gates of Buckingham Palace, Tony Threadgold said, "'Oo's inside the coach then?"

'How on earth would I know?' snarled the Queen.

The image on the television screen changed to

show a Japanese frigate passing under Tower Bridge. Sailors, British and Japanese, were lined up on deck, saluting. The Queen snorted contemptuously. Then suddenly the picture changed again to show the balcony of Buckingham Palace where two tiny figures appeared. The camera zoomed in to show that one was Jack Barker, dressed like a lead soldier in a war game. He was wearing a tricorn hat with a white plume and a scarlet jacket, hung with decorations that the Queen couldn't identify. The person standing next to him was the Emperor Akihito, resplendent in a silk kimono.

They waved to the crowd below and the crowd automatically waved back. Then Jack stepped to the left and the Emperor stepped to the right and two more figures appeared, one in a shimmering confection of white silk and chiffon and a headdress trimmed with orange blossom. The other in grey morning dress, complete with top hat.

'Who the hell is *that*?' shouted the Queen. The camera obligingly closed in even more to show her. It was her son, Edward, glassy-eyed and unsmiling, holding the hand of his new bride, Sayako, daughter of the Emperor.

The Queen watched incredulously as the Emperor smiled at his new son-in-law and Edward bent forward like an automaton and kissed his new wife. The crowd below cheered so loudly that the Queen's television vibrated.

'They've hijacked Edward!' raged the Queen. 'He'll be forced to live in Tokyo as *her* consort!' The Queen jabbed her finger against Sayako's image on the screen.

She had already taken against her new daughter-in-law.

Her head was filled with a roaring sound, like thunder. The camera switched to show the sky over Buckingham Palace with the empty flagpole in the foreground. Overhead, the former Red Devils, now resprayed yellow, screamed into view and executed daring twists and rolls over the palace, delighting the crowds below. Edward's glum face watched as the aircraft disappeared over South London.

And then it happened. A flag slowly inched its way up the flagpole and flapped arrogantly in the wind. It was the Japanese flag. The Queen shouted, 'Has the world gone completely bloody *mad*?'

Sayako, supported by Edward, was bending down and appeared to be lifting something she hoped would endear her to the millions of watching animal-lovers. When she straightened up, the camera moved over to show what it was that Sayako held under her arm. It was Harris, wearing a collar trimmed with orange blossom.

'Harris! You cowing little traitor!' screamed the Queen.

Harris gazed sycophantically up at Sayako. The Emperor put his hand out to pat the little British dog. Harris bared his teeth and began to snarl. The Emperor foolishly persisted in his attempt to pat the dog's head but before he could do so Harris had snapped irritably at the Imperial thumb. The Emperor struck out at Harris with a glove and instantly lost the sympathy of the entire watching British public.

Harris bared his teeth in a malevolent grin and

then began to bark furiously. The camera continued to close in on Harris until his head filled the screen. The Queen and her visitors drew back in alarm. All that could be seen were Harris's sharp teeth and his red, liver-coloured tongue.

52 The Morning After the Night Before

The Queen woke with a start. Harris was jumping up and down in front of the television set barking with record-breaking ferocity. She was drenched in sweat. The heavy linen sheets pressed on her, clammy and cold. She looked, as she always did, towards the damp patch in the corner but it had gone and had been replaced by what appeared to be a fine silk wall-covering. 'Oh do be quiet, you cowing little dog,' shouted the Queen.

Harris continued to bark at the empty screen. To shut him up the Queen found the remote control and turned the television on. It was the morning of the tenth of April 1992 and a red-eyed David Dimbleby was wearily repeating that the Conservatives had won the election.

'Oh God, what a nightmare!' groaned the Queen and pulled the sheet over her head.

Sue Townsend

ADRIAN MOLE: THE WILDERNESS YEARS

This completely new volume from the celebrated diarist picks up where *Adrian Mole From Minor to Major* left off. Adrian Mole, now aged twenty-three and three-quarters, is a gloomy lodger living disconsolately in the box room of the brilliant and beautiful Pandora's Oxford flat, spurned and barely tolerated by his former boyhood sweetheart. He is still working at the Department of the Environment with special responsibility for newts – a species he has come secretly to loathe.

Sue Townsend's new book charts another two and a half years of frustration in the life of the world's most famous misunderstood genius. It is not certain that he will achieve any of his New Year's Resolutions in 1991 – or even in 1992. But these diaries of the self-pitying underdog will undoubtedly win him still more fans in this further worm's eye view of life in middle England.

ADRIAN MOLE:
FROM MINOR TO MAJOR

Adrian Mole: From Minor to Major brings together the three bestselling volumes of Adrian Mole's diaries for the 1980s – *The Secret Diary of Adrian Mole Aged 13¾, The Growing Pains of Adrian Mole* and *True Confessions of Adrian Albert Mole* – with Adrian's previously unpublished diaries for 1989 and 1990. For the first time between the covers of one book, these are the complete Adrian Mole diaries, taking him from 13¾ to 23¾.

'It seems set fair to become as much a cult book as *The Catcher in the Rye* ... Both touching and screamingly funny.'

Jilly Cooper
on *The Secret Diary of Adrian Mole Aged 13¾*

'Adrian Mole was first introduced to the British public 10 years ago. Since then he has established himself as a classic ... The Adrian Mole diaries are, in fact, thoroughly subversive. They constitute an attack on all the half-baked ideas on marriage and parenthood that have been cheerfully swallowed by middle-class trendies for the past 30 years or so ... A true hero for our time.'

Richard Ingrams

Stephen Fry

THE LIAR

Stephen Fry's breathtakingly outrageous début novel, by turns eccentric, shocking, brilliantly comic and achingly romantic . . .

'A quite brilliant first novel'

Sunday Times

'*The Liar* is hilarious – page after page of the most outrageous and often filthy jokes, delicious conceits, instant, brilliant ripostes that would only occur to ordinary mortals after days of teeth-grinding lunacy'

Literary Review

'Brilliantly entertaining and consistently outrageous'

Daily Mail

'It's very unfair. It took Joseph Heller seven years to write *Catch 22*. Stephen seems to have knocked this one off on a couple of wet Wednesday afternoons in Norfolk.'

Hugh Laurie

'Sublime'

Cosmopolitan

Sue Limb

SHEEP'S EYES AND HOGWASH

'The plot of *Sheep's Eyes and Hogwash* is corn of the finest grain. Polly is a Hampstead career girl staying in the country to gather material for a TV adaptation of *Cold Comfort Farm*. At first, appalled by rural society and homesick for the "sweet, dry, fragrant pavements of Knightsbridge", she is slowly seduced by the charms of the countryside and a swain called Swain . . . Limb's obvious competitors are Joanna Trollope and Jilly Cooper. Her instinctive appreciation of the countryside runs deeper than either's'

Sunday Telegraph

'Highly entertaining . . . If you take this book on holiday you will probably finish it on the flight'

Sunday Express

David Nobbs

FAIR DO'S

Since his disastrous elopement with the ravishing Liz Rodenhirst in *A Bit of a Do*, what hope has Ted Simcock with his new waitress friend, Sandra?

Can his ex-wife Rita find fulfilment with her Social Liberal Democratic candidate?

And can the marriage between Liz and the immaculate Neville Badger possibly succeed?

David Nobbs provides the answers to these and many other questions as Rita, Ted and Liz pick their way through social minefields of more sublimely ridiculous 'do's', including a fancy dress party, the opening of a vegetarian restaurant and a funeral.

A Selected List of Fiction available from Mandarin

☐	7493 1352 8	**The Queen and I**	Sue Townsend	£4.99
☐	7493 0540 1	**The Liar**	Stephen Fry	£4.99
☐	7493 1132 0	**Arrivals and Departures**	Leslie Thomas	£4.99
☐	7493 0381 6	**Loves and Journeys of Revolving Jones**	Leslie Thomas	£4.99
☐	7493 0942 3	**Silence of the Lambs**	Thomas Harris	£4.99
☐	7493 0946 6	**The Godfather**	Mario Puzo	£4.99
☐	7493 1561 X	**Fear of Flying**	Erica Jong	£4.99
☐	7493 1221 1	**The Power of One**	Bryce Courtney	£4.99
☐	7493 0576 2	**Tandia**	Bryce Courtney	£5.99
☐	7493 0563 0	**Kill the Lights**	Simon Williams	£4.99
☐	7493 1319 6	**Air and Angels**	Susan Hill	£4.99
☐	7493 1477 X	**The Name of the Rose**	Umberto Eco	£4.99
☐	7493 0896 6	**The Stand-in**	Deborah Moggach	£4.99
☐	7493 0581 9	**Daddy's Girls**	Zoe Fairbairns	£4.99